A MOST FORTUNATE LIFE

by James H. "Buck" Harless

International Standard Book Number 0-87012-810-8
Library of Congress Control Number 2011962824

Printed in the United States of America

Copyright © 2012 by James H. Harless
All Rights Reserved

Printed by
McClain Printing Company
Parsons, West Virginia
www.mcclainprinting.com
2012

*In celebration of
family and friendship.*

Dedicated to Mom.

*With heartfelt thanks to Gary Simmons for
his extraordinary help in writing this book.*

Foreword
by Gene A. Budig

Buck Harless, whose mother died soon after his birth, was raised by his Aunt Rosa and Uncle "Ras" in the small town of Gilbert. Rosa, whom he called Mom, was a strong-willed woman who typified the strength and sensitivity of southern West Virginia.

Even though the family was poor, Buck always felt very fortunate. He saw Rosa especially as blessed with the highest values, most of which he adopted throughout his life. Rosa was always willing to lend a helping hand to many friends and neighbors who were in need. She was fearless and lived her life exactly as she believed in her heart. She taught Buck at an early age that the color of one's skin does not matter, when the family took in a Negro named "Shorty" after he had been seriously injured in a construction accident. Shorty was the only black in Gilbert, but he became a valued member of the family and eventually of the town. Buck grew up during the Great Depression and remembers his family often sharing a meal with a hungry stranger or two.

At age 12, Buck Harless embarked upon his first business venture, collecting scrap metal that he found along railroad tracks and elsewhere and selling it to the junk man for pennies. Being a natural entrepreneur, he recruited his friends to join him and generously shared the profits. When mothers in Gilbert noticed their iron skillets and aluminum pots were missing, the burgeoning business came to an abrupt end.

Buck worked at the town's only garage and was taken by the honesty and integrity of its proprietor, George Crago, a master mechanic. Buck always loved cars, especially the fast ones, a trait that would follow him for a lifetime. He drove a school bus when he was a junior and senior in high school and a wrecker for Crago's Garage.

He had only one run-in with the law when, as a teenager, he saw fit to tell the town policeman that he was being too rigid with his daughter, a good girl and student. The exchange of words became charged and nearly resulted in an altercation. "As always, Mom took my side but with little reason to do so," Buck recalls.

Buck was a very good student, making only one B over his entire academic career. While he graduated high school, he couldn't afford to go to college. In those tough times, half of his classmates dropped out of school. Because school played such an important role for him and everyone growing up in Gilbert, Buck and others started a popular high school reunion that briefly swells the town's population with returning classmates who are happy to reminisce about earlier times.

Harless eloped with his high school sweetheart, June Montgomery, in 1939, much to the chagrin of her father. He went to work in the coal mines as a laborer, a tough but well-paying job at the time. "We kept beating that rock hour after hour, while the superintendent stood or sat nearby, holding a light for us," Buck recalls. "I often thought I wouldn't make it through the day." Before long, he gained a position in the company's engineering department.

Buck Harless got into the lumber business, becoming a

partner with two others who owned a rundown sawmill. He soon bought out his partners, and his one-man operation faced a daily struggle to survive.

Buck and June Harless had two children, a son, Larry, and a daughter, Judy. His mom died shortly after Judy's birth, and Buck remembers being devastated.

Buck loved his family, but too often he veered off the track, partying and womanizing. One evening, when his life was an emotional shambles, he found spiritual renewal at the Gilbert Presbyterian Church. In 1955, he and his wife and daughter were baptized and a new chapter in his life began, and he became a good husband and very attentive father to his son and daughter.

He and son Larry ran a growing and profitable lumber business, building mills in Brazil, Ecuador and the Appalachians and selling their products throughout the world. They became close as father and son and as business partners. Daughter Judy, a lover and trainer of horses, made a home in Tennessee with her two girls.

As a businessman in coal and lumber, Buck became very successful and influential, using genuine humility and an uncanny ability to bring people together to work to enhance the common good in West Virginia and elsewhere.

He has a long line of acquaintances, associates and good friends, but Fred Shewey is his closest friend. They would do anything for each other.

When June Harless died after a long illness, grief and loneliness wore on him for an extended period. He later married Hallie Chapman, whom he had known for years. Hallie is an independent woman, one of 10 children, a successful businesswoman in her own right and a former teacher with two degrees in education from Marshall University.

Buck has been active in politics since the first gubernatorial campaign of Cecil Underwood in the 1950s. He was finance chairman in West Virginia for George W. Bush, who carried the state in the 2000 presidential election. West Virginia's five electoral votes were enough to give Bush the Electoral College win, and the new president claimed that Buck Harless was the reason he won the election.

Even though Harless never went to college, he has five honorary doctoral degrees, including ones from West Virginia and Marshall universities.

The state's largest newspaper, *The Charleston Sunday Gazette and Mail,* a publication that he often disagreed with on editorial policy, selected him in 1983 as "West Virginia's Man of the Year."

As a former president of WVU, I knew Buck well, often marveling at his ability for objective thought and unflinching commitment to give back to other deserving souls. Since we share values, we have remained close over the years and seek the other's counsel on sensitive issues. He continues to support both athletics and academic programs at WVU.

Buck Harless is 92 years young and filled with insight, the kind that matters to all of us today.

Gene A. Budig has been president/chancellor of thee major state universities (Illinois State University, West Virginia University, and the University of Kansas) and Major League Baseball's president of the American League. He has three degrees from the University of Nebraska.

Preface

I have never claimed to be a writer, and I don't know if anyone will be interested in reading about my life. I confess that others have put me up to this, particularly a fine lady named Sharon Murphy, who has worked for me and with me for a number of years. She has prodded me for some time now to put down on paper my recollections of events and people who have contributed to a rich, gratifying and sometimes painful life.

When I reflect upon the past, I'm warmed and humbled by the good, dear friends that I've had the pleasure of knowing over a span of nine decades. I recall my childhood and the love provided me by an aunt and uncle who volunteered to be my parents after my mother died. I remember my classmates and teachers and the simplicity of growing up in the wonderful little town of Gilbert, deep in the rugged hills of southern West Virginia.

I think of the decent man who gave me my first paying job, while at the same time, instilling in me the honorable way to do business and helping to open my eyes to a much bigger world. I think of my naiveté while growing up, of being paddled twice in the same day by the same teacher and of sassing a Gilbert police officer.

I think of adulthood and marvel at how fast the days have flown by. I remember my strength and determination to work long hours day after day in order to gain success in the business world. I remember successes and failures, and I'm amazed that I could have failed as often as I did, yet still have had many opportunities to succeed.

Aren't my memories like yours, especially if you have a few decades of experience yourself? And, if you're young like my great-grandchildren—whom I wish I could see more often—what do you care of memories other than your own?

I count the days—the tens of thousands of days—that the good Lord has given me on earth, and I'm thankful for every single one of them. But I know that the gift is not endless. Perhaps that is why I reflect and attempt to put lasting words on paper; it might be a way to share even when I'm no longer here.

I know that I don't want to embellish or suggest that I'm someone I'm not. Warts and all will be my motto because there is no perfection in the human spirit, certainly not in mine. I hope that you gain an insight or two from my experience, which you might use on your own path through life.

I've already mentioned Sharon Murphy who initiated this project. I want to acknowledge others who have given much-appreciated, wide-ranging assistance with special thanks to Gary Simmons. I would also like to acknowledge Meg Andrews and Debra Burgess. And thank you to McClain Printing Company in Parsons: Michelle Mullenax-McKinnie, Kenneth E. Smith, Kevin White and others who produced this book.

James H. "Buck" Harless
November 2, 2011

Chapter One

Southern West Virginia is central to my life story. I was born there, I grew up there, and it's where I live today.

My family, as I was growing up, is somewhat hard to explain. When I was four months old, I was taken to be reared by my mother's oldest sister, Rosa. My mother, Bessie Brown Harless, had been so weakened during my birth on October 14, 1919, that she developed pneumonia and died in the cold of January. She was only 22 years old. I have no memory of her, only a photograph of her in her youth and the stories that Aunt Rosa told me. In her illness, my mother exacted a promise from her sister: to take me to raise if she didn't recover. Rosa kept her promise. As the story was told to me, when Rosa and "Ras" came to take me to their home, they came by train. While we were boarding for the return trip, I soiled myself and began wailing. Ras tried soothing me, and as he did, he called me Buster. The name stuck. Even though I was born James Howard Harless, from that day forward and throughout my childhood I was known as Buster Ellis. (It was not until the end of my high school years that I was given the nickname "Buck.")

My father, Pearly J. "P.J." Harless, and my mother already had two children before I was born. We were all split up after my mother passed away. My older sister, Mae, went to live with my father's relatives in Charleston. My older brother, Fred, remained with my father, who moved on to South Point, Ohio. My brother and my sister rarely visited me, so I didn't get to know them until I was older.*

I had other brothers and sisters too. My father had been married once before his marriage to my mother. That marriage produced three children: Milton, Frank and Marie. My father's third marriage was to Lizzie Trent, and they had nine children. They made their home in Gilbert, except for a brief time when they lived in South Point.

Rosa and her husband, George Erastus Ellis, whom everyone—including me—called Ras, provided me a loving home. Rosa was always Mom to me. I called her Mom because she was in every way my mother. I considered myself so fortunate, since no child could have had a more loving and devoted mother.

Mom and Ras first took me to their home in Davin, where Mom ran a clubhouse, a boarding house for miners at Powelton Coal Company. We lived there until I was about three years old, when we moved to Gilbert, a little town along the Guyandotte River, where I have lived ever since. It has just a few hundred residents, so it is a place where everyone knows everyone else. Its citizens are generally good people, who are good neighbors and good friends.

The first house we lived in was a big, old three-story affair, which sat at the mouth of Stafford Branch on the outskirts of town. It had about 14 or 15 rooms, certainly more than we could use. We stored boxes and old furniture in a few of the rooms, and the others remained empty altogether. Some of my earliest memories are of that house. To my young mind, it had an unpleasant character because it seemed strangely alive, perhaps even haunted. I rarely took the time to investigate it in its entirety and preferred always to stay in the most familiar rooms at night.

Before I entered grade school, we moved to another house in the middle of town, right across the highway from the grade school and high school. That house became the anchor of my life throughout my childhood and even after I got married. When I think of my childhood, most of my memories are centered there. That was home. (The house burned down when I was about 25 years old and living on my own. The fire consumed everything, not only the building, but the photographs, keepsakes and memories that involve the prompting of touch and smell. I've often wished that I could return to that house, if only for a short time.)

I can close my eyes and see the old kitchen table where my family ate every meal. In the kitchen were the mismatched dishes and coffee cups, which were mostly free promotional items from a gas station or a detergent box. What we called silverware was anything but silver. Mom did her best to spruce things up by covering the rough top of that old table with a floral-patterned oilcloth.

Our house had been built in two sections at two different times. The original structure was a two-story log house, which was very small and crowded. Ras, who was a carpenter among other things, built that log house in the early 1900s, long before he and Rosa were married.

The old part of the house was very solid. Downstairs there was a living room and kitchen, and upstairs there were two bedrooms. The kitchen was big enough to serve as the dining room as well. It had an old table with eight chairs around it, and in one corner of the room, there was a big coal stove with four lids and an oven. We had a fireplace in the living room and another in a bedroom above the living room. The fireplaces and the kitchen stove provided all of the heating for the house. The only cooling we had in stifling summer heat were little oscillating electric fans. We had drop-cord lighting, really nothing more than a small light fixture hanging from an electrical cord dangling from the ceiling.

The new section made the house into the shape of an "L", and a porch ran the length of both sections. Like so many others in southern West Virginia, our house was built against the side of a mountain. A porch from one of the second-floor bedrooms extended out onto the lane that passed behind the house and up the mountain.

The addition consisted of four bedrooms, two downstairs and two upstairs. I can tell you that it could be cold in those bedrooms. I slept in one on a featherbed with numerous blankets and quilts piled on, and that made it possible to stay warm while I was in bed. On a really cold morning, however, it took genuine gumption to hit the cold floor, dress quickly and race to the kitchen, where Mom had already fired up the cook stove, which gave off good heat.

We used both wood and coal to heat and cook, and we got the coal from a coal bank, an exposed seam of coal along the hillside up the hollow from our garden. We dug the coal right out of ground and used a wheelbarrow to bring it back to the house.

Like everybody in Gilbert, we had an outside john, otherwise referred to as an outhouse. For the uninitiated, an outhouse is a primitive toilet facility: a simple wooden shed built over an approximate three-by-four-foot hole about eight-to-10 feet deep. Ours was a fancy "two-holer," which sat around the hill a short distance, so the odor would not find its way back to the house. Outhouses worked reasonably well, and only occasionally, we would add lime to help cut down on the stink.

Mom took care of the whole extended family on only $25 a month. With all those mouths to feed, including hungry transients who were passing through, we didn't have a whole lot to eat at any one meal. Mom was not only a good cook, she was a great manager. She could make a dollar go a long way, and I can tell you that I always had enough to eat growing up. She was the one who would make do with less, never once complaining or letting on that she had sacrificed. Sometimes there was very little food on the table, but it was always enough. By far the most valuable things Mom had in the kitchen were her iron skillets. She always said that you couldn't make good cornbread unless you did it in an iron skillet, and Mom made the best cornbread.

At the dinner table, Mom sat at the end nearest the stove and I sat to her right. "Vertie" (Alberta), Mom's daughter from an earlier marriage, would sit beside me. She was several years older than I and had children of her own, Doris and Jack, who stayed with us too. Sometimes, Ras's son, George, lived with us and he would sit beside Ras at the other end of the table. Ras had four boys before he married Mom, but George was the only one of his sons who ever lived at home while I was there.

In this day of fast food at every corner, it may strike some younger people as hard to believe, but we rarely ate meat. Sunday was an important day meal-wise because we could look forward to having chicken and dumplings. The other big meal day was Saturday, when Mom made terrific hotcakes. (I had friends who played sports with me in high school, and they would frequently spend the night. In cold weather, Mom would have a bunch of hotcakes waiting for us in the morning. We'd eat heartily, joking and having a good time. The boys always enjoyed staying with us because Mom treated them right.)

Our primary source of food was what we grew in our garden. We had a little garden in back of the house where we grew tomatoes, cucumbers, lettuce and the like. Up the road a piece, Ras owned some property in the hollow, and he raised a big garden there. I'd go with him sometimes, after much urging, to hoe a little corn. But not very often!

Gardens were a mainstay then, but it is so different today. With times as they were, a garden was a necessity. Today, even people on welfare or those with very little money rarely bother to raise a garden. The art of gardening is being lost to all of us, and it's a real shame, since there's usually some place around where a person can supplement what he has by growing his own food.

We killed at least one hog every year, and it was a big deal. Neighbors came to help, and someone in the group was a skilled butcher. They heated water, then scalded and scraped the hog's hair off before butchering. After salting the meat, they took it to the cellar, an icehouse that had been dug into the side of the hill in back of the house. It was really a man-made cave with block walls and blocks of ice. It wasn't cold like a freezer, more like the cool of a refrigerator. The salted meat stayed good enough to eat for quite some time. After the meat preparation, they made soap out of the hog fat, which was used to wash clothes.

When I was a kid, almost everyone had a cow. We had a cow, and Mom taught me how to milk it. I didn't do it very often, but she taught me nevertheless. To tell you the truth, I wasn't exactly enthusiastic when it came to that kind of work. I loved sports, and I loved to build things. I was an extremely active boy. But gardening and milking? I just didn't see much going on there. In fact, I generally did absolutely nothing to put food on the table. To be honest, I watched while others butchered the hog, never did the laundry nor helped much around the house. If you have the impression that I was pampered child, I would have to agree. I will tell you this: I was a very happy child.

During my youth, most of the houses in Gilbert did not have indoor plumbing, and each house had a well for water. Mom insisted that I clean up before each meal, but that was no simple task. I'd go to the well, pump a bucketful of water and carry it back to the house before I could splash cold water on my face and wash my hands. For bathing—usually once a week on Saturday—we pulled out a big metal tub, heated the well water on the cook stove and bathed either in the kitchen or on the back porch. Once I got a little older, since we lived right across from the high school, I took showers there after football or basketball practices. In the summer, I even sneaked into school to take a shower, even though there was only cold water when school wasn't in session. I wasn't always able to take showers at school, but I greatly preferred even a cold shower to that metal tub

We were poor like most everyone else in Gilbert. In the summertime, I wore overalls and ran around barefoot. In the cold and wet seasons, I wore shoes, but I owned only one pair. When holes wore into the soles, I placed sturdy cardboard inside the shoe. In fact, I was always on the lookout for good cardboard to extend the life of my shoes. Many of us kids in Gilbert used cardboard in our shoes because our families had no money to repair the shoes properly, much less buy new ones. I had only two sets of clothes that I wore to school. While one outfit was being worn, the other was being washed and readied for the next change. Of course, I didn't change outfits but every few days. We made do in any number of ways. For example, when we played ball, we rarely had a real softball or baseball. Instead, we'd take yarn, wind it into a ball and cover it tightly with black tape, and it worked just fine. I learned it doesn't take a lot of money or material possessions to have a happy childhood.

Our front yard faced old route 8, which is U.S. Route 52 today. Old route 8 made a 90-degree turn just past my house. In the 1930s, the state bought a little land from Ras to straighten out that severe curve. After the improvement, the road was renamed U.S. Route 52, although it remained a dirt road until World War II. It may surprise some people that a major artery which connected points south to Cincinnati, Indianapolis, and all the way to Chicago, was not paved, at least the section through West Virginia wasn't.

I remember that everyone in town was excited at the prospect of an improved highway. They thought it would open up the town for commerce and bring lots of visitors. Mom had many conversations with the local politicians about the potential of the highway upgrade. Politicians liked to talk to her because she had a reputation for being direct and knowing what people wanted. The consensus was that the upgrade of the road was the beginning of great things for Gilbert, but it didn't happen.

Unlike Mom, Ras didn't get involved with politics. He was a very unassuming person, and I dare say that he was henpecked. I say that as a kind of joke, but there was no doubt that Mom was the boss in the house. Ras loved Mom dearly, and he was just happy to go along with what she said and did. If there was anything that I wanted, anything at all, if he was able to give it to me, he did. He'd go out of his way to see that

I got the first tomato out of the garden and stuff like that. As far as he was concerned, I could do no wrong. He was like Mom in that regard. I never gave him enough credit for the generous way he treated me over the years. As I look back, I can see that he was pretty outstanding.

At one time, Ras was a deputy sheriff in Logan County under the notorious Sheriff Don Chafin. He worked for Chafin during the infamous Battle of Blair Mountain. He told me that what happened up there was greatly exaggerated. He said there were lots of guns and quite a few people threatening to make war. He allowed that there was a lot of shooting, but it was generally at night when nobody could see anything. And although people were killed, he said it wasn't nearly as bad as many people have claimed.

When I was about 10 or 11 years old, my knees would ache and hurt, and the pain was hard to bear. Ras would sit with me for hours, gently rubbing my knees to soothe the pain. He would talk to me in a low, soft voice and ask me if this or that made it feel better. He was a gentle, good-hearted person.**

Mom was a very determined, strong-willed woman with quite a temper. She was also very loyal to those she loved. She was one of 17 children, all with the same father, although there were two mothers. She was a member of the Brown family from Huff Creek, a family which was quite prolific. In fact, I have 51 first cousins on the Brown side.

While Mom was a disciplined woman, she was also one of the most compassionate people I've ever known. It was not unusual for her to care for the sick throughout the night or even for days at a time. She cared for sick friends and for those she hardly knew. We had a town doctor and also a nurse named Miss Ward, who performed many duties similar to a doctor. Even though we called her Miss Ward, she was married to the town dentist, a man who stayed mostly drunk and useless. Miss Ward was a fine old lady, who cussed like a sailor. She delivered a lot of babies around here and helped a lot of people, including those who could not afford to pay for medical care. Mom assisted her in a variety of situations. Miss Ward didn't own a car and walked to appointments, sometimes for miles, to help people in need.

On occasion, Mom would spend a great deal of time away from home tending to the needs of others. Being a kid and wanting attention, I couldn't understand why she would do it, and I'd make snide remarks that I'm sorry for now. Today I think of how she'd come dragging home early in the morning, having been up all night nursing someone with a serious illness. She was always doing for others.

In those days, a person who did those kinds of unselfish acts of charity would certainly have been considered religious. Mom did not look upon herself as a religious person, however. She had been baptized years earlier at her old home church, Claypool Methodist on Huff Creek in Logan County. She went to a revival sometimes, but she didn't attend church regularly. She got no pressure from Ras in this regard because Ras never went to church period. I'm pretty sure he was never baptized, and he never showed any interest in such matters. Mom was a person who lived her religion by her actions and by the way she treated others. Today that's known as the social gospel, but for Mom, it was a matter of simply doing the right thing. It wasn't in her to turn away people in need.

Since we lived on the main highway in Gilbert during the Great Depression, we saw people traveling any way they could: walking, hitchhiking or in weighted-down cars, carrying with them all of their possessions. There were all kinds of transient visitors all the time. Hungry, desperate people, they came knocking at our door, and Mom would invite them to stay and eat. We rarely sat down for the evening meal when there wasn't a stranger at the table, and sometimes there'd be people at lunch too. More than once—in fact, many times—I watched her put a second helping on a stranger's plate when she knew there wouldn't be anything left for her to eat. That's what I call charity, and that's one of the many things I learned from Mom. Welcoming those who need help into your home is a loving and respectful thing to do, and you should always find a way to feed hungry people.

When the Norfolk Southern Railroad was built through Gilbert in 1932 and '33, there were a number of jobs available, but the rates of pay are hard to fathom from today's perspective. Common laborers were paid 10 cents an hour; truck drivers got 15 cents an hour, and shovel operators made 25 cents an hour. John "Shorty" Tatum was one of the laborers. He came here from Lynchburg, Virginia, to work for J.W. Walters Construction Company, which had the contract to build the section of railroad through town. He got his nickname because he was just four feet eight inches tall.

Shorty was seriously injured on the job when he fell into a pit where large rocks and debris were being dumped. Those big rocks damaged him severely, and he spent over a month in the hospital at Welch. Once he was discharged, he was not fully healed from his extensive injuries and had nowhere to go. Mom heard about his dilemma and offered to bring him to our home to convalesce. That's how Shorty came to live with us. When Mom died years later, he still lived with her and Ras, and her passing hurt him as much as it did any of us.

I should point out that Shorty was black, and at the time, he was the only black person living in our community. In 1932, it was a rare occurrence for a white family to invite a black man into its home to live, but that was Mom for you. She was going to do the right thing no matter what others thought, even though she suffered scorn and ridicule for a time. Shorty adored Mom, and to show his gratitude, he helped around the house and worked at other little things she needed done.

I got a lot of kidding in school for having a black man living at our house, but Mom straightened that out right quick. "He's just as good as you or I or anyone in this town. Just remember that."

I can still hear her ask, "Shorty, are you ready to eat?"

"Yes, Mom." She made a place at the table for him, but he never sat with the rest of us. He waited until we were finished.

If he was slow to come to the kitchen after we ate, she'd say, "Shorty, you get your butt in here! It's time to eat."

"Yes Mom. Yes Mom." He was always polite and spoke very slowly with a deep southern accent.

He liked to drink wine, and sometimes he would imbibe too much. His room was next to mine, and I remember one night as he noisily came home tanked. I could hear his unsteady navigation of the stairs, and it sounded as if he made two steps up and one step back. All of a sudden, I heard this loud thump and jumped out of bed to discover that he had fallen off the second-story porch onto the yard.

I ran to where he lay motionless. "Shorty, are you all right?"

"Yes sir. Yes sir," he answered meekly in a voice from the Old South.

"Are you hurt?"

"No sir. No sir."

Surprisingly, he had fallen about 12 feet but broke no bones, although he was quite sore for a few days.

Shorty was an integral part of the family for 14 years. After Mom died, the community built him a little house so he could stay in Gilbert. Sid Hatfield, who owned a grocery store, hired Shorty to carry out groceries for customers, and everybody in town came to love him because he was a very decent, humble person.

One day Sid came to me and said, "Buck, I'd like to see Shorty be able to visit his family in Lynchburg. Will you help pay for some good traveling clothes and railroad tickets?" We got Shorty all decked out in new clothes and supplied him a round-trip ticket. I drove him to Iaeger to meet the train. When Shorty returned, he told this story:

"I got off the train in Lynchburg at night, and I went to my sister's house because I knew where she lived.

I knocked on the door, and my sister says, 'Who's there?'

I says, 'It's your brother, Shorty.'

She says, 'Get away from here, n-----. My brother Shorty's been dead for years.'

'No, I swear. This is your brother Shorty.'

'I told you, get away from here, n-----.'

'Do you remember when you scalded me with hot water? I can show you...'

Then the door opens, and she says, 'Lord have mercy. It is my brother Shorty!'"

Shorty visited his family for about a week but came back to Gilbert because it had become his home. Shorty lived for another 15 years after Mom died. One day a neighbor found him dead in his little house. He's buried in our family cemetery, and I put flowers on his grave every Memorial Day.

* I was 14 the first time I saw my sister, Mae. My brother, Milton, brought her to Gilbert to a dance at the old beach along the Guyandotte River. After that I saw my siblings more frequently.

There was a beautiful sandy beach along the Guyandotte in Gilbert. In fact it was so beautiful that the C&O Railroad had a special Sunday train in the summertime that brought passengers from Huntington to the beach for the day. The train parked on a side track, and bathers sunbathed and swam throughout the day. At 6:00 p.m. the locomotive's whistle blew, signaling that it was time to begin the return trip to Huntington. Everybody loaded up, and off they went.

On Independence Day, there was a big celebration at the beach with an orchestra and fireworks. One year, two orchestras performed, one from 2:00 to 6:00 p.m. and the other from 8:00 p.m. until midnight. It was a big deal, and folks came from all over. Tickets were $5 a couple, and hundreds attended, even in the midst of the Great Depression.

Fred came to live with us in Gilbert during his freshman year of high school, and we fought all the time. I think he was jealous of the way Mom treated me, and I was jealous of him just being there. I don't believe that we really despised each other; we were just being kids.

As an adult, Fred became a successful coal operator. After he retired from the coal business, he was killed in an airplane accident just outside of Gainesville, Florida. Attempting to land in bad weather, the pilot, Gary Cline, made a serious miscalculation and flew into a television tower. Gary's brother in law, Larry Walls, was in the plane as well, and all were killed instantly.

** Many years later when I got into the lumber business, Ras worked for me measuring and grading logs, something he knew very well. He was in hog heaven working at the sawmill. He was happy to help me in the business, and there never was a better worker in any of my operations. Every day, he was the first man on the job and the last one to leave.

Chapter Two

It is interesting to reflect upon the happiness of my childhood and to see that luck played a big role in it. My Aunt Rosa's and Uncle Ras's willingness to take me into their home and make me their child was one of the luckiest things that ever happened to me. Another big piece of luck was living directly across the highway from the schools where I received my education, so I can't tell hardship stories of trudging through heavy snow for miles to and from class. The grade school and high school sat side by side, and I only had to walk across the road to get to either. School was not only the place where I gained an education, but it was where I found friendship, athletic training and a satisfying social life.

I sometimes wonder how different my life would have been if I had lived miles away from school. Ras used to tell me how he would walk six miles in each direction to a one-room schoolhouse. He continued that routine throughout frigid winters, doing chores at home before and after school each day. To be perfectly honest, I'm not sure that I would have been as diligent and disciplined as Ras had been.

My childhood was much easier. I didn't have much to do in the way of chores, so I energetically threw myself into just about everything that school had to offer. I was a sports-loving, good student with friends galore, and I applied myself to those pursuits without hesitation. Some of the kids had difficulty doing all these things because they lived so far away. Some had to walk a good distance to and from school, while others were forced to curtail after-school activities because they had to ride the bus. The school system provided bus transportation to kids from outlying areas, and when that final bell rang, you either got on your bus or faced a long walk home. Football practice conflicted with those bus schedules, and if you were a kid from an outlying area who played football, you had to be very dedicated. Today, almost everyone owns a car, but in 1920s Gilbert, automobiles were few and far between. The idea of parents picking up their children after school was unheard of, and no high school student in Gilbert owned a car.

In fact, cars were so scarce that one of my earliest measures of success was to own one. I started dreaming of having my own car when I was about five years old. I thought that owning a car one day would prove that I had made it, and that Mom and Ras would be really proud of me. I would imagine sitting in the driver's seat of my big, shiny automobile, driving around town and being greeted by friends and townspeople, who would look upon me with respect and adulation.

Indeed, my fascination with cars led to one of my most vivid, though least pleasant, childhood memories, and I couldn't have been more than seven when it happened. There was a new car in town, and it belonged to Roy Fox, who was the president of the county board of education and a leader in the Democratic Party, so he was pretty well off. The first time I saw his car, I was sitting on the steps of one of the town's gathering places, the Ellis Restaurant. Mr. Fox and his son, Alton, pulled up and parked right in front of me and went into the restaurant to eat lunch. I was consumed by the presence of this strikingly beautiful automobile and simply could not contain myself for long. Barefoot and wearing my trademark overalls, I nonchalantly ambled over to the car to admire the magnificent machine. I examined the sweeping fenders, the white-walled tires, the delicate spoke wheels and the mesmerizing new car shine. After going over the exterior from top to bottom, I decided that I needed to investigate the interior, so I opened the door and plopped myself down in the driver's seat.

I hadn't had the chance to fully appreciate the delicious aroma of the interior, when Alton Fox, a teenager twice my size, yanked me from the car and threw me to the ground. I can still hear his voice as he glared down at me, "I'll kick your ass! Don't you ever do that again. Look at you, you dirty little rat!" It was as if he was a member of some very exclusive, members-only club, who was addressing a mangy dog.

I've never forgotten that moment, and through the years, I've had many opportunities to pay him back for that bit of ugliness. But I never did because I learned that carrying a grudge can make it difficult to go on with your life. I've known quite a few people who have had their lives dominated by deep-seated grudges. Still, I've never forgotten what that Fox boy did to me way back in 1926.

Most of my early school memories revolve around a typical school day. Once awakened on a school morning, I'd hesitate only a moment to collect my thoughts and prepare myself for the shocking cold floor of my unheated bedroom. I was motivated to move quickly not only by the cold of the room, but by the aroma of breakfast: eggs frying and bacon sizzling. I was always hungry, so I did not let wardrobe decisions get in the way of my stomach. Besides, I could practically jump into my overalls.

After dressing, I'd tear through the house to get to the kitchen, where I'd stand near the stove to warm myself before taking a fast, chilly trip to the outhouse. Back in the kitchen, I'd gulp down breakfast. Mom would give me a quick inspection, pat my hair down with her wet fingers and check to see that I was fully prepared to head off to school, and across the road I'd dash.

In grade school, it took a little longer to get up and off to school because I would take the time to sit down and eat breakfast. By junior high, I gave up the sit-down breakfast for a few extra minutes of sleep. By high school, I could accomplish the entire procedure, from bed to school desk, in under 15 minutes, although personal hygiene and a balanced diet suffered in the process.

I loved school, not only because it was the center of social life, but because I loved to learn. I loved all of the subjects, but I particularly loved books. Books opened the world to me, and I was interested in learning all that I could, so I read and read and read. In the higher grades of elementary school, the teachers held reading contests to see which pupil could read the most books during the school year. Rather than just claim to have read the books, we had to give a report on each one as proof. One year I won by reading 38 books.

I read novels, principally westerns, which to this day I still love to read, but I also loved history books and biographies. I have always been sort of a history buff, so I read Hawthorne, Melville, Twain and Zane Grey. And I have always been fascinated with the Civil War, so I read about Gettysburg, Antietam and Appomattox. (My son Larry also loved history texts about the Civil War, something that he picked up from me.) I'm not sure why I gravitated towards the Civil War, but I think it might have to do with the fact that it was so important to West Virginia's statehood.

I wasn't then, nor am I now, an especially fast reader, but I was highly motivated: I wanted to learn. By grade school, I had become accustomed to the way of life in Gilbert, and without books, it would have been hard to fathom how life could be any different from what I happily experienced every day. But books took me to different worlds and introduced me to big cities, enormous plains, vast seas and desert mesas.

I'm in my ninth decade, and it surprises me to note that inside I feel the same as I did when I was a child. By and large, I have the same internal identity that I did then. When I read today, it's the same as when I read as a child. I believe a person's internal being is the same throughout life, and it's our physical being and memory that change so dramatically.

I would bet anything that the school library of my day had a better selection of books than what is available in small schools today. But today's schools have what nobody in my classes could have imagined: the Internet, a virtual world at your fingertips through the World Wide Web. Back in the 1920s and '30s, a Zane Grey or a Mark Twain novel stimulated my imagination and allowed me to see the world—in my mind's eye at least. Today there's not one kid in 20 who reads books or much else. When they're not out riding around in cars or doing something away from home, they spend much of their spare time watching television or surfing the Net. Today, if a youngster is at home, it's safe to bet that the television is turned on and a computer too. In my youth, we had to seek out things to do.

As a child, I marveled at the world and still do. What is so different now is the amount of information that's available. The typical second-grader nowadays knows more about the world than most adults gained in a lifetime just a few generations ago. This additional knowledge has its consequences, both good and bad. I think it's reasonable to ask if a seven-year-old should have so much information at his fingertips—much of it adult oriented. These advancements in technology are definitely remarkable, but I think that many kids today grow up too fast. And the advent of the personal computer and its derivatives has only magnified the access to information and increased both the positives and the negatives available to any child.

My wife, Hallie, is a teacher, and some of the things that she's told me about her pupils are hard to grasp. Much of their bad behavior is attributable to what they see on television. What do they watch? Many times shows that are meant for adult viewing. If a family subscribes to cable or satellite TV, a kid can flip on the television and watch programs loaded with violence and sex—and worse. Even on the over-the-air channels, there are hundreds of references to sex, from jokes in sitcoms to broken-hearted testimonials on talk shows, or on the latest craze, reality TV. I think that's wrong, and something needs to be done about it. Part of the problem is that the parents won't monitor what their kids are doing, and even though there are devices to block such programs, few people use them. If the government tries to do something, the issue of freedom of speech comes up. Although it is a serious subject that has to be considered, I don't think our Founding Fathers meant to accept these circumstances when they guaranteed freedom of speech and freedom of expression.

Television is an important invention that has changed the world in fundamental ways. In certain instances, it has absolutely harmed our young people. Kids are in terrible physical shape these days, even though we know more about nutrition than ever before. Their pathetic physical condition is from lack of exercise because they sit for hours staring at the "tube." They don't even have to get off the couch to change the channel! I know I'm not alone in my ambivalence toward television. On the one hand, I think it's wonderful, even though I don't think it is being used properly. This is probably a silly statement: I think we'd be better off without television. I've learned that reading a good book is far superior to watching TV—unless it's a West Virginia University football game.

Just as the Internet is the hot, new medium of today, radio was the hot, new medium of my childhood. Wirt Hatfield was the first person in Gilbert to own a radio. It may have been a gift from his father, Uncle Ed Hatfield, who owned a shoe repair store. We considered Ed Hatfield pretty well off because shoe repair was a big business in those days as not many people could afford to buy new shoes. Even though Ed's shop was tiny, he was able to establish himself as one of the most successful people in Gilbert. His hands stained brown and black by leather dyes, Ed was a reserved old gentleman, who was not very talkative. While he wasn't the most sociable fellow in town, on certain occasions, his house was the most popular, all because of his son Wirt, or more specifically, all because of Wirt's radio.

After Wirt got his radio, folks dropped by the Hatfield's more frequently. They'd say things like, "Just happened to be in the neighborhood...," or "Thought it had been a while since you and I...," or "The neighborly thing is to check-in on your neighbors once in a while..." Ed was always his characteristically quiet self. I'm sure he saw right through the charade, but he wasn't one to protest or speak out. He knew that visitors had come to marvel at Wirt's radio, so he joined in, sitting on the front porch with Wirt and the others—and the prized radio.

Wirt would tune his battery-powered radio set to an AM station in Pittsburgh, Pennsylvania, KDKA, the first commercial radio station in the United States. Since the technology of radio was so new, KDKA was the only station that the few people who owned radios could tune in for a long time. We'd all gather around to listen to the big events. There was one big problem: Wirt's radio did not have a speaker, so we only heard Wirt describe what he heard through his headphones.

I vividly remember the night of a Jack Dempsey-Gene Tunney fight. There must have been 50 people gathered around the Hatfield's front porch listening to Wirt call the fight blow by blow. I should note that Wirt had the same quiet reserve as his father and was no big talker. Sadly, Wirt wasn't much of a sportscaster either, and his rendition of the fight did not exactly transport his eager listeners to ringside in Chicago. Wirt's portrayal of the fight went something like this: "Dempsey just hit Tunney." Then after a long pause, he'd blurt, "And Tunney hit Jack!" There'd be another long pause, and all of us would be on pins and needles waiting to hear more description of the action.

Someone would yell, "Come on, Wirt, tell us what's going on!" It was excruciating and exciting at the same time trying to glean from Wirt what was happening with the fight. None of us really knew whether he portrayed the fight correctly or not.

It was the immediacy of it all that made radio so attractive. We knew it was clearly more than a passing novelty. Gilbert was suddenly connected to the rest of the world, and we became aware at the same moment as events unfolded thousands of miles away—well, with minor delay, compliments of Wirt Hatfield.* It took a few years before the rest of us heard actual broadcasts through radios with speakers rather than headphones. Only then did we learn just how well radio sportscasters could make a fight or a ballgame come to life with their lively play-by-play descriptions and commentary.

I was fascinated with radio, but I was much more interested in cars. While it was a real treat to be exposed to radio programs, it was only on special occasions and for big events that radio was truly memorable. On the other hand, automobiles were a daily fascination. When I was 11 years old, I could wait no longer: I just had to drive. So, for reasons I no longer remember, I decided to take the family Plymouth on a little ride to Man, a town about 12 miles from my house in Gilbert. I don't even recall why I decided to drive to Man and not somewhere else.

The story of my early car "thievery" has been told more than a few times, and it seems that with each telling, my reported age gets younger and younger! Some renditions have me as young as seven, but I'm setting the record straight right here: I was 11.

Even at 11, I had to practically stand up in order to reach the pedals and see through the steering wheel. On my getaway, I had to cross an extremely narrow bridge down by the old bank building, where the Bank of Mingo is currently located. The bridge had been built in the first part of the 20th century for horse- or mule-pulled wagons. It was narrow and a tight fit for a car with just a few inches to spare on either side. There were no side rails, so if you missed your mark, you could go over the edge for a 40-foot plunge into the cold river. Many cars drove across that bridge without problem through the years, and today, I wouldn't give it a second thought. But for an 11-year-old joy rider in a stolen Plymouth, it was frightening! With heart thumping, I negotiated the bridge, and then gleefully set my compass for the far off town of Man.

When Mom couldn't find me or the Plymouth, she let her imagination run wild and soon concluded that a band of Gypsies had kidnapped me and stolen the car. That may sound like wild conjecture, but her thinking had a somewhat logical basis. There had been reports of Gypsies traveling through Gilbert at the time, and stories of Gypsies stealing cars, household goods, dogs and even children. I never actually knew of a Gypsy stealing so much as a wooden nickel, but these stories were wildly repeated whenever they made an occasional appearance in the area.

These mystifying people travelled in groups, in jalopies pulling over-sized trailers or wagons, some of which were the strangest-looking homemade rigs. Their caravan of vehicles would crawl up the mountains as slow as a man could walk and roll down the other side, jostling and careening at dangerous speeds.

The Gypsies made no attempt to hide their culture, which seemed so entirely different from our own. They wore colorful clothing like hippies in the 1960s and '70s. The men sported large loop earrings and studs of diamonds. The women had several piercings in each ear and earrings of gold and multi-colored jewels and diamonds—or at least we assumed them to be jewels and diamonds; for all we knew, they could have been glass or rhinestones.

Wild stories circulated when they camped for the night along the river at the edge of town. People swore that they heard the Gypsies making crazy sounds and loud and boisterous music. Some folks even claimed to have seen them dancing as if they were cavorting with Satan himself!

When the Gypsies passed through, townswomen pulled their children a little closer to them and warned them to not stray too far when they played outside because, "The Gypsies will get you." I'm not sure what we thought the Gypsies would do with the children once they had stolen them, but with the reputation that we attributed to them, serving the children up as the main course at dinner would not have been too far-fetched in our minds.

Perhaps you can see how Mom put two and two together and also understand that her conclusion was enough to make her crazy with fear. She told anybody who would listen that she would find and kill anyone who hurt her little boy in any way, and she meant it absolutely. Three or four hours later when I casually drove back into Gilbert after experiencing the ride of my young life, Mom was both relieved and angry. She didn't hit me with a belt or a switch. Nor did Ras lift his hand in anger. Mom did, however, sting me as effectively as beating me with a switch: she gave me a most intense tongue-lashing, something at which she was highly skilled.

Once it settled in her mind that the Gypsies had gone along their merry way without stealing her boy or the Plymouth, Mom relaxed somewhat. Seeing that I was both unscathed and sorry for my ill-conceived actions, she hugged and hugged me until I thought I would just about suffocate. Then she pushed me back and told me that I would be the death of her, running off like that for who knows what reason, and she surely would punish me to show me that she meant business. Then she looked at me and realized again that I was OK, pulled me back into her arms and hugged me once more, while I sought to pull away as boys of 11 are prone to do in response to so much affection. I don't remember what my actual punishment turned out to be. For grand theft auto, I'm certain that I got off pretty lightly. In that era, boys were sent away to correctional facilities for a whole lot less.

Thinking of that car and my joy ride raises a significant question. If we were so poor, how could we have owned a car during the Depression? While everything I've told you about our poverty is true, I have to theorize about the car ownership and propose a plausible explanation, which may or may not be true.

During my youth, certain people made good money selling moonshine. Of course, it was illegal to do so, and anyone involved kept very tight-lipped about their activities. I recall that Ras's son, George, was nearly caught once hiding half-pints of whiskey in a cornfield near a dance hall in Gilbert. I have a few vague recollections to suggest that Ras had a hand in moonshine and that George may have been his salesman. I doubt that their activities went very far since George had been almost caught. We really had so little to live on in general, but moonshine may explain the Plymouth in the garage.

In the fifth grade, when I turned 12 years old, I came down with typhoid fever. It nearly took me out, and I slipped in and out of consciousness for a month.

Two doctors told Mom and Ras that my condition was hopeless and that I was going to die. Fevers at that time were very hard to control, since there was no penicillin or any of the wonder drugs we have today. Once a child had a fever of 105 for more than a day, the odds of recovery just weren't good. It was not uncommon for households to lose a child or two due to various childhood illnesses such as typhoid fever, scarlet fever, rheumatic fever, measles and mumps. These were killers before modern medicine.

Mom simply refused to accept that I would be taken by a fever, and she sat by my bed practically the entire 30 days and nights. She was defiant toward my illness and about my prospects for survival. She wasn't going to let it beat me or her. She forced me to take sips of water and juices. She broke open raw eggs and made me swallow them whole to provide nourishment. Apparently, I had enough will to live that I co-operated even in my battered state. Every time I opened my heavy eyes, even just for a moment, I saw Mom sitting there. I felt her petting me, stroking my hair or wiping my burning brow with a damp cloth. Sometimes, I accept that the doctors had been right, that there was no real medical hope for my survival. I think it was Mom who pulled me through in spite of the odds. I don't know that I would have made it without her. This was the first time I cheated death, but it wouldn't be the last. I suppose it's not unusual to have had a close call or two by the time you reach my age.

I've told you how much I enjoyed school and that I was a good student. More truthfully, I was a good student most of the time. I didn't go out of my way to cause trouble, and I wasn't the teacher's pet. I rarely got into any trouble with my teachers or with other students.

I was only spanked twice the entire time I attended school, and both of those swattings came on the same day, the very first day that I went back to school after recovering from typhoid fever. It had rained fairly heavily the night before, and at recess, all the kids were playing and running through the schoolyard's mud holes and water puddles. I was right there with them, splashing and getting soaked in return.

Mr. Lonnie Cline, the principal, was on schoolyard duty, and when he saw me splashing away, he yelled, "Hey, Buck, you quit that! You've been sick, son. Quit!"

Dutiful as ever, I stopped, but as soon as he turned his back, I started jumping and splashing again. In my exuberance, I lost track of Mr. Cline, but he did not lose track of me. He walked right up to me from behind, gave me a yank and whipped me on the spot. Ouch!

Wounded and embarrassed, I went back to class. My teacher, Miss Blankenship, became really upset with Mr. Cline. I admit that I may have milked the situation for pity, but she also sympathized greatly with me since I had been so sick for so long. She simply thought that he did wrong by me. I don't know if she said something to him or if he had second thoughts on his own, but at noon Mr. Cline tried to make up with me. And what was my response to his peacemaking attempt? I rebelliously sassed him. So right back upstairs he took me and whipped me again, harder this time. The only two whippings I received in school took place in a two-hour time frame. It was a highly unusual day.

My life, until I was about 13 or so, was as easy flowing as the Guyandotte River. In retrospect, those years had almost the feel of a Mark Twain novel. Like the boys in his books, my friends and I would laze by the side of the river and watch it gently flow by. The Guyandotte was pure and clean then. While there were coal mines in the area, there were no coal washers to muddy the river like today. Also, people took care of their sewage in outhouses; they didn't pipe it into a creek to have it carried away downstream as is the all-too-common current practice.

We fished a lot in those days. Sometimes, we gigged fish, even though it was against the law. To gig fish, the water had to be clear in order to see them. The best time of the year to gig was when the fish swam up river to spawn. At those times the water was full of fish and we used a three-point spear on the end of a pole, speared the fish and then scooped them up.

We would also trap fish, which was also illegal. Ras was good at making effective traps. He'd take a certain kind of a white oak, saw it into quarter-inch strips and make traps with a funnel at one end. Once a fish got into the trap, it couldn't get out. My goodness, I've seen him raise those traps and 50 to a 100 fish would be wiggling in an almost solid mass. Those traps would be chocked-full, usually with big cat fish.

The game warden had a home along a section of the river that was ideal for trapping, and Ras would push his luck by setting and emptying traps at night right near the game warden's house. One night, after much begging on my part, Ras took me and a buddy along with him to check the traps. We moved along in darkness very carefully and quietly. When he pulled up one of those traps, it was so filled with catfish that it sounded as if someone was hitting a boat with a paddle. Those squirming fish made such a racket! We saw a light come on in the game warden's house, and Ras quickly set the trap back into the water. It was a close call, and Ras later made certain to empty his traps when the game warden wasn't at home.

Ras and his son, George, who was at least 15 years older than I, would go up Gilbert Creek in the spring when the fish would be migrating for their annual spawning. George and Ras would gig them as the fish swam upstream. My job was to carry a big sack, and as Ras and George would gig the fish, I'd place them in the sack. Sometimes, I'd end up with a sack so full that I couldn't carry it. That's how thick those fish were in that clear, cool creek. Either George or Ras would relieve me of my burden, and victoriously, we'd go home to Mom, who fried those fish up. I can still hear the sizzle of that hard-earned meal in the frying pan, and I tell you that those fish made for an extremely tasty and satisfying meal.

---

* Wirt Hatfield used good grammar, and his mastery of English in general was excellent because he was married to the English teacher all of us had in the fifth grade, Thelma Blankenship. She was a real fanatic about using proper grammar and spelling. She would drill all of her students over and over again, imprinting proper grammatical constructions. I don't pretend to retain great mastery of grammar or of English rhetoric, but any proficiency I have began in her fifth-grade class. To this day, I find myself thinking through phrases or sentences based on her valuable lessons from almost 80 years ago.

Wirt Hatfield later became the principal of the grade school, an elder and treasurer in our church and one of Gilbert's most prominent citizens. But he was surely never more popular than when he had the town's first radio.

Chapter Three

It is impossible to pin down the exact moment when the innocence of childhood transforms into the worldliness of teen youth. Is it the first job? The first trip far away from home? The first automobile accident? Within a two-year period, I experienced all these things and more.

The transition actually began at age 12 when I started my first business and suffered my first business failure. It all began by collecting old scrap metal that I found along the railroad line and other places, which I took to the junk man, who paid me a few pennies per pound for it. It didn't take long for me to embrace the notion that scrap-metal recycling had great income potential.

Soon I expanded my little business by bringing in additional staff: friends to whom I offered cash for the metal that they found. I'd give them half the rate that I received from the junk man and take the other half as my fee. Business boomed, at least for a couple of weeks. I suspect that, at its high point, half the kids in Gilbert were scouring every nook and cranny looking for metal that I would redeem for cold, hard cash. I know I was certainly busy overseeing a small army of young entrepreneurs and making several profitable trips to the junk man.

What happened next was worse than the crash of '29, at least for me and my partners. Several mothers noticed that their iron skillets and aluminum pots were missing, and they got very upset. It took no great detective work to focus suspicions on me and my new business, and needless to say, my venture crashed almost immediately. It was a play on the old story of supply and demand. The mothers cut off the supply by demanding that no one touch their precious metal household items.

My cousin, Vertie, wanted to learn to drive. Since I was 12 and fully checked out in the family Plymouth, I offered to share with her some of my driving knowledge and skills. So, with Vertie behind the wheel, I riding shotgun in the front passenger seat and Vertie's two children, Doris and Jack, tagging along in the back seat, we set off on dirt-based, rutted U.S. 52 for Vertie's first driving lesson.

It soon became apparent to me that my cousin had little appreciation for the subtleties of driving a car. In fact, she was scaring me to death. She kept steering too close to the right edge of the road where there was a really deep ditch, and I feared that she would drive into it. It must have dawned upon her that she was flirting with disaster because, all of a sudden, she steered the car hard in the other direction toward a creek, which was 40 feet down a steep slope from the left side of the road. I grabbed the steering wheel, hoping to ward off catastrophe, but Vertie fought back hard, having her own ideas on how best to correct the situation. The Plymouth heaved right, then left, then right again, tossing the two children in the rear seat back and forth, as if they were a couple of oversized melons.

I was fighting mightily to keep our out-of-control Plymouth from going into the creek on the left or crashing into the cliff on the right. When we wrecked—oh, we wrecked alright—it was directly into the cliff. We couldn't have hit that rock face more surely or squarely, even if we had aimed directly for it.

The Plymouth lay mortally wounded on the road, totaled by the 35 mile-per-hour impact, and I was knocked out and bleeding profusely from my head. Vertie nursed an injured leg and the kids were scared silly but otherwise uninjured. When I came to, I frantically tried to flag down a car to take us to Dr. Walker's office, but no one stopped to help at first. Three or four cars passed us by before a guy named Childers finally came along in his new sedan and offered to take us to the doctor. During the trip, I bled all over his new cloth interior, and at the end of the ordeal, I had 21 stitches in my head and much regret that I tried to teach my cousin to drive.

When I was 12, I started spending more and more time at Crago's Garage next door to our house in Gilbert. This should be no surprise, since I was obsessed with cars, engines and all things mechanical. A fellow named George Crago had set up shop there after appearing in town out of the blue. He came to Gilbert at the beginning of the Great Depression. He just showed up one day in his car with his wife, his young daughter and all of his earthly belongings. His car was in tip-top condition, and the trunk was full of mechanic's tools. Why he came to Gilbert, I never really knew, but I do know he wasn't running from anything. He had been roaming around looking for a place to set up shop when he found Mom's old building, which she rented to him for $25 a month. That rental income was how our family of seven survived through three years of the Depression. Crago put in gas pumps and other equipment and turned that old place into Gilbert's premiere gas station and garage.

George Crago was a man who made a big impression on me. At six feet three inches, with straight black hair and high cheekbones, he was half-Cherokee. You might think that the people in town would have been a little suspicious of a fellow who just dropped in out of nowhere, and initially, some in town were a bit skeptical of him, but once they got to know him, they were won over. He was quiet and reserved, an unassuming man of tremendous integrity, and he was an excellent mechanic, who worked very hard, developed an excellent reputation and built a good business.

Even back in the 1930s, there were plenty of mechanics around who would not claim further responsibility for a vehicle once it left their garage. There were unscrupulous tradesmen of all types, just as there are now. But Crago was an extraordinary exception: he absolutely guaranteed his work. He was my first businessman role model, and I couldn't have chosen a better one.

I found myself often hanging around his garage, leaning against a tool chest and taking in the sights and sounds. In the summer, I'd spend hours there, and sometimes Crago would ask me to fetch a tool as he worked under a car, something I was pleased to do. Heck, if I had had the money, I would have paid him for the opportunity just to be part of that atmosphere. It would have been like paying tuition to learn a trade and to study and understand how to succeed in business.

Later on, he gave me a job working for him in the summertime. I started at 25 cents a day, a pittance even then, but I saw it as a chance to learn from the town's best mechanic. I began each day by opening the garage at 7:00 a.m. By the time Crago came in a half an hour later, I had already swept the place and would be replacing any tools that were lying around, trying to keep things as tidy as possible.

Throughout the day, I fetched tools, greased cars, and held parts in place when Crago needed that third hand. I pumped gas by hand—electric pumps were a decade away—checked the oil, ensured that tires had proper inflation and washed the car's windows. A service station in those days was truly all about service and not about selling milk, bread, lottery tickets or beer to its customers. When Crago finished a repair, it was up to me to wash the car and give it the best shine possible. He was particular about making sure that the cars looked as good as they ran.

My favorite part of working for Crago was when he allowed me to drive him around town, usually to pick up a customer's car or, less often, to grab a bite to eat. I loved my role as Crago's chauffeur since I loved to drive. Crago talked very little during those trips because I did the talking for both of us. I'd make observations about the town and surroundings as we drove, or talk about a particular mechanical problem, asking him how he had managed to figure it out. He'd always answer but with few words. He wasn't stingy with either his information or his friendship: he was just an extremely quiet man. He was the epitome of the strong, silent type, which was the model of a solid American man during the 1930s.

Crago taught me a lot of things that have stayed with me ever since. Honesty and integrity were essential to him; they were his hallmarks. If he worked on a car, he guaranteed the repair. Sometimes, he'd overhaul a motor, which was a big job, and if it didn't work perfectly, he'd do it over at his expense. People trusted him because he earned their trust. There are some in business who believe that power is the key to success. Crago taught me that trust and mutual respect are the best ways to deal with your fellow man and that honesty and integrity will carry you a long way, even when times are tough.

He became like a second father to me. Occasionally, we'd go bowling, a bonus of sorts, like picnics and Christmas parties that companies throw for their employees. While most of those trips blur together in my mind, one was quite memorable.

We had gone bowling in Logan and were having a sandwich between games, when this drunk came in looking for trouble. He sat down near Crago and me, glared around the room, then back at Crago and said, "Hey, buddy. I'm the meanest son of a bitch in Logan."

Crago said nothing.

"I'm the meanest son of a bitch in Logan!" the drunk bellowed, wild-eyed and menacing.

Again, Crago said nothing.

Finally, the drunk got up, stood over Crago, gave him a shove and yelled, "I'm the meanest son of a bitch in West Virginia!"

In an instant, Crago stood and hit the drunk with a solid right. The force of the punch was so great that the drunk reeled across the room, crashed into the far wall and landed on the floor, knocked out cold. "I figured you were a son of a bitch," Crago said to the drunk, in an even voice. "But, now I know where you're from."

I must have been bug-eyed at the sight of Crago's one-punch knockout. I know I gained another valuable lesson: understatement and action are far more effective than talking big and having no plan of battle.

George Crago was the most generous man I had ever met, and I can recall many of his kindnesses. But there is one particular instance in which he expanded my world view in a very big way. I have often felt that this remarkable act of kindness and selflessness greatly helped me in my earliest ambitions to succeed in life.

The world's fair took place in Chicago in 1933. I guess I had heard about it at the time, but to me the distance from Gilbert to Chicago compared roughly to that from here to the moon. I didn't pay too much attention to this far-away event. It was like most of the things that happened in New York or California, which we heard about on Wirt's radio. It was part of the other world that took place far, far away from Gilbert.

In real terms, the distance was extraordinary. There were no interstate highways, and many of the national highways were still dirt roads, bumpy and impossibly dusty or muddy depending upon the season and the weather. Automobiles were not nearly as reliable as today. In spite of all of these obstacles, Lon Cline, the school principal, decided to take his family to the Chicago World's Fair. One day he brought his car to the garage to have Crago make sure it was ready for such an arduous trip. I must have been all ears when Mr. Cline described his upcoming journey. I am sure that I was keenly interested, as if I had been listening to The Lone Ranger on the radio. It seemed incredible that the Cline family was going to the World's Fair.

There I stood, grease gun in hand, black streaks on my face and arms, a dirty rag hanging from my pocket, totally mesmerized by Mr. Cline's descriptions. When he asked me if I'd like to go along, you could have knocked me over with a feather. I learned in an instant the meaning of the saying, "Even if you can't dance the cha-cha, it sure is fine to be asked to the dance." That moment of exhilaration quickly gave way to the harsh realities of life. "Mr. Cline," I answered, "it sure seems like it will be a mighty fine trip, but the truth is I don't have money for something like that."

Crago looked up in his calm way and told me to go home and start making preparations for the trip. He said that he would provide the money for me to go to Chicago, and he followed through on his promise. He gave me $50, an absolute fortune to a kid of limited means in those days and a great deal of money to just about anybody in Gilbert.

I went with the Cline family to Chicago to see the world's fair. In addition to Crago's gift, Lon and his wife, Iva, helped a great deal too by taking care of the room and board for the entire trip. I bunked with their son, Ralph, and family friend, Maurice Ellis. I recall staying in a motel in Indiana and lying in bed unable to sleep with countless thoughts of new things to come. As I lay there in the darkness, I heard a train whistle that came from miles away because I could barely hear it. That sound so far in the distance reminded me of how far away from home I was, and in a moment of apprehension, I thought to myself that I'd never make it back home to Gilbert.

To travel across the great Midwest, with land so flat that it seemed that you could see forever, was an enormously eye-opening experience. The open spaces were startling to someone like me, who was so familiar with the closed hollows and steep hills of the Guyandotte Valley. As amazing as those open spaces were, however, they paled in comparison to the great metropolis of Chicago. I had never imagined anything like it with its huge, tall buildings and thousands of people rushing every which way. I had been able to picture the world through books and radio, but to actually be in the midst of this thriving city was stunning.

Lon and Iva rented a small apartment in Chicago. Ralph, Maurice and I slept in a room separate from the grownups. I had a cot and the two boys shared a double bed. We saved money by cooking our own food in the little kitchen with only an occasional restaurant meal. Since Lon and Iva paid for the room and the food, it really helped me to stretch the money that Crago had given me, and I made every penny count.

We took in every exhibit, pavilion and show that we could pack in. People ask me what I remember from the 1933 Chicago World's Fair, and I always tell them that I recall vividly a mechanical perpetual-motion machine and fondly the discovery of cotton candy. I don't always tell them that I remember something else clearly and a little painfully: I was turned away from seeing the world-famous fan dancer Sally Rand. What made it painful was that Ralph, who was three months younger than I, got in to see the show along with the men because he was already shaving, and I was exhibiting little more than "peach fuzz." That bothered me immensely, but it didn't spoil the great time I had otherwise.

By the time we made it home, I had just 35 cents remaining of that $50 gift and memories to last a lifetime. The trip with the Clines* gave me a wonderful glimpse of the larger world outside of Gilbert and its ancient, familiar mountains. It whetted my appetite for travel and for accomplishment, and it showed me that I could go out into the world, even to a city the size of Chicago and travel back to Gilbert unscathed. It taught me that there may be things to be cautious of, but there is nothing, utterly nothing, to be afraid of. George Crago made all of that possible: an enormously enlightening experience through a single act of generosity.

When I turned 14, Crago helped me to get a driver's license. The law required that a driver had to be at least 16, and he took me to the exam and swore to the state police testing officer that I had just turned 16. Crago needed me to have my license so that I could lawfully drive his wrecker to accidents and the like, and of course, I had wanted a license forever.

Crago's wrecker business had its harrowing moments. I recall responding to a wreck on the other side of Justice, where a LaSalle and a Ford Model A roadster had crashed head on. Crago and I went to the scene together, and our initial investigation showed that the driver and passenger in the Model A had been killed on impact. The car was so mangled that it took awhile for us to discover a third fatality in the rumble seat. The three people in the LaSalle were seriously injured, but there was no ambulance service to take them to the hospital.

A fellow by the name of Bob Woolridge owned a station wagon, and we took the rear seats out of his vehicle and transported the injured to the hospital at Williamson. On the way, we could hear groaning from the rear of the station wagon, but when we got as far as Pigeon Creek, we no longer heard the groaning. We quickly stopped and checked on our passengers and discovered that one of them had died. We raced on to Williamson with the remaining two, who survived the ordeal. It was quite an event for a 15-year-old to experience. I tended to several nasty car wrecks with Crago and his wrecker, but none as gory as that.

By the time I was in high school, Crago would loan me his 1930 Model A Ford so I could take young ladies out on dates.

His generosity in that regard is quite impressive and was sincerely appreciated, since it would've been impractical, if not impossible, for me to date girls without a car.

Crago's marriage failed while he was in Gilbert. His wife quietly left town, but he stayed for a time with his daughter. Later he married a Gilbert girl, and sometime after that, he set up a new shop in Logan and a while later, one in Princeton. From Princeton, he moved to Blairsville, Pennsylvania, where he opened a truck stop.

We kept up our friendship over the years, and he called me one day after I had had some success in business. "Buck," he said, "I'm having a bit of a rough time. I've got a good business going here, but I don't have enough cash flow to buy the inventory I need. Would you be able to loan me $10,000?"

I was happy to help him, so I sent him a check with the intent of making it a gift. But he insisted on paying me back, and in about a year, he did just that, repaying the $10,000 in full. It was yet another act of honor and integrity from a dear friend and teacher.

When my daughter Judy was to be married, I invited Crago to the wedding. He was eager to attend, but he was living in Pennsylvania and was a little too old to make the long drive by automobile. I sent a plane for him, and he visited for an entire week. He came to my church and stayed to hear an informal talk that I made about what my faith meant to me. We reminisced about the old days, the times at his garage and the people we knew. He was married yet again, this time to a wonderful woman named Norma, who was a school teacher in Pennsylvania. Crago clearly adored her, and they were extremely happy. I think he felt settled for the first time in his somewhat nomadic life.

In 1977, George Crago passed away, and I went to his funeral. After he was laid to rest, I was at his house talking with his daughter. "I have something for you," she said, "something that I found in Dad's wallet. It's a little worn, but I think you'll remember." She handed me a small dog-eared photograph, a picture of me taken in 1928. Crago had carried that picture with him all of these years.

When I think of the most important people in my life, I am lucky—actually blessed—to be able to name quite a few, but George Crago is near the top of that list.

---

* There was a tragically sad end for Lon and Iva Cline, two educators who gave so much to students from the Gilbert area. Upon retirement, they planned to spend time in Florida. Prior to their departure south, they scheduled physicals with a doctor in Welch. On the way to doctor's office, they crashed head on with a coal truck. Lon died instantly, and Iva died the next day.

It was a devastating loss for this community. I delivered the eulogy at their funeral. There were hundreds in attendance, which is not at all surprising given their long service to area children. I reminded those in attendance that there was no need to rush out and build a monument to them, that enduring monuments already existed in the hearts and minds of thousands of their former students.

Chapter Four

Cromer's Drug Store was one of the best hangouts in Gilbert. It wasn't really a pharmacy because they didn't fill prescriptions; it was actually a soda fountain that also offered necessities like iodine, Goody's Headache Powders and other over-the-counter basics. Lots of little communities had a place like Cromer's.

The kids in town loved to gather there, and those of us who were lucky enough to have a quarter could buy a sandwich—Cromer's served the best chicken salad sandwich that I've ever eaten—and a Vanilla or Cherry Coke. With a dime more, you could finish off your meal with an enormous sundae. My favorite was pineapple; to this day, I love a good pineapple sundae. Some things never change.

If we didn't have any money, we would just hang out with the others and shoot the breeze. Mr. Cromer was a kind and very tolerant man who didn't care if we had money to spend or not. (Mr. Cromer and I became pretty good friends. In fact, I got to know his entire family and was especially good friends with his only boy, Sonny, who was three or four years younger than I. Sadly, Mr. Cromer was an alcoholic, and drinking would ultimately kill him.)

Cromer's Drug Store sat right next to the high school. You can imagine the activity there after school let out. We could generate a lot of noise and occasional disorder. Generally, however, we were fairly well behaved, and I don't remember a time when an argument ever led to a ruckus inside the place. If trouble seemed to be brewing, someone would shout, "Take it outside!" I guess none of us wanted to risk damaging our favorite hang out.

Cromer's had a Nickelodeon, an early form of a jukebox, a big wooden and chrome machine with lights running up the side and over a curved window, through which we could watch the records being lifted from their rack and placed on the turntable. With its bright, colored lights and luscious music booming from its speakers, that Nickelodeon just made you snap your fingers and tap your toes.

Mr. Cromer must have been excited about having a Nickelodeon because, when he put it in, he cleared a little room where we could dance. A young man with only a dime in his pocket could take his girl to Cromer's, buy her a Coke, hang out with friends, play a meaningful tune on the Nickelodeon, escort her out onto the floor and make her the center of attention by dancing to delicious music. Of course, most boys and their girls would just sit at the counter or in a booth, nursing a Coke, each using a bent straw to sip from an authentic, flared Coca-Cola glass.

The girls loved to dance, but most of the boys weren't too eager. I, on the other hand, always loved to dance. I'd take a nickel and drop it through the coin slot, listening for it to make its path to the collection box, when the buttons would light up. Then I'd press G-12, E-7 or something similar and watch the mechanical sorter find the selection. By the time the record was placed on the turntable and the needle set down on vinyl, I was already on the floor, partner in arm, ready to dance. The music of Tommy Dorsey or Benny Goodman's orchestra would fill the room with magnificent instrumental sounds. Or Bing Crosby's voice would croon, and I'd press my girl closer to me during a slow dance. While the other boys sipped their Cokes, I was on the dance floor swinging and swaying my troubles away.

Most of our troubles in Gilbert had to do with a lack of money. During the Great Depression, of course, most of America was broke, but in Gilbert, we were more broke than most. Since a fellow couldn't dazzle his girl with expensive dates or luxurious gifts, he'd have to be a little creative. Mainly—as boys do anywhere—he'd have to get up the gumption to simply ask the girl out.

Back when I was dating, a girl would never approach a boy for a date or even directly indicate that she wanted to go out with him. It was always up to the boy to develop a plan, gather the courage and make the first inquiry. Often that wasn't done quite as openly as it could have been. Instead, he might ask his sister or a cousin about a girl he had his eye on, and his go-between would work her contacts seeking information about the girl and her intentions. After amassing useful intelligence that confirmed the young lady in question held similar feelings, it was still the boy's obligation to find the nerve to ask her out.

Today some girls are much more assertive, and what they sometimes do is just unbelievable to me. I'm not saying that all girls are this way, and I know that it's a different world today and a very difficult time to grow up. I know, too, that young people see disrespectful presentations of sex and other forms of immorality at an extremely early age through all of the media sources. In any event, some of them are more aggressive and interested in partaking of things that we didn't even know existed when I was a youngster. For example, I never heard of oral sex when I was a kid. Maybe I was simply naïve, but I think I was typical of my generation. Even through high school I remained unaware.

We had a few bus trips when I was in high school, and I won't pretend that we were all hands-off and lily pure. During a nighttime bus ride back home from some extracurricular event, we would neck, kiss a little, and maybe even try to feel a girl up. If you were going steady and had been dating for a long, long time, maybe she would allow you a little bit of a feel of her breast through her blouse, of course, never against her brassiere and certainly not flesh against flesh. That was as far as it went mostly. A few of the kids would go further and some of the girls would get pregnant before they graduated, but, by gosh, we didn't couple up in public places as some do today.

Having made a comparison of the past and present, I should point out that my first sexual encounter took place when I was 14. My partner was a woman twice my age, although I was the initiator. She was a live-in worker for a family in Gilbert, rather attractive and a bit plump. It was satisfying, but not altogether so, and we did not become a couple.

Throughout life, I have tried not to be boastful, but in the ninth grade, I made a boast that caused me to be ridiculed by my friends, even though the reason for making it was easy enough to understand. I was always in need of money, and even small amounts were invariably in short supply, so the chronic frustration of not having money led me to tell Mom that I was going to be a millionaire by the time I reached the age of 40. Mom, who supported me in every way possible, told me that I could do it if I really believed and worked at it. She was the only one to give credence to my boast. Word got out, and I was harshly chided more than once. I became sorry that I ever made such a claim. Ironically it came true, but Mom didn't live to see it.

In high school, I was chosen by the principal to go to each classroom every morning to check attendance. One of the teachers, Miss Ridgeway,* who had come from Louisville, Kentucky, to teach in Gilbert, had a very difficult time maintaining discipline among some of her students, namely Rufus Buchannan, Bud Wingo and Ray Perry. When I approached her room, I was always careful to open the door, just a crack at first, because I was never certain if one of those troublemakers might try to hit me with a paper wad, eraser, chalk or worse.

One morning I carefully opened the door and saw her at her desk, tears streaming down her face and the boys running roughshod over the class. I ran back to the principal's office to report the uprising. He pulled the three boys from her room, took them to his office and whipped them really hard. Even a good whipping had little impact on those three, and they were back to their pranks the next day.

When I was 15 or 16, I took up smoking. Most kids of high school age smoked back then, but not everybody stayed with it. My preferred brand was Wings and they were 10 cents a pack. While I have not suffered from tobacco to the extent that many have, I can tell you that taking up smoking was not a smart thing to do.

Almost all of the kids drank a little beer but not all the time. I drank beer too, but I never let Mom find out. I had a friend named Doris White, who could knock down a beer better than most guys. We'd get beer for 10 cents a bottle at her aunt's restaurant, The Golden Arrow. She'd drink one, and sometimes two, for every one that I'd drink and never get up to pee. I don't know how she did it.

I had my one and only drink of moonshine at a young age. My friend, Rouhier Spratt, and I went to visit his girlfriend at a Christmas party at War Eagle. There was some moonshine on the table along with a bowl of hard candy. Someone poured me a drink and I took a slug. It was awful! My mouth and throat burned so badly that I grabbed for a piece of candy to try to extinguish the blaze in my throat and stomach. The candy was powerless against the awful burning, and I got deathly sick. To this day I can't stand the taste or even the thought of moonshine.

I drove a school bus when I was a junior and senior in high school. Even though there were two bus routes, we had only one bus, a Dodge. We used a truck to transport the kids from Isaban and War Eagle. My route, which took upwards of three hours to complete, went to Horsepen, down to Verner and up to Steel in Wyoming County. (Some kids from Wyoming County attended school in Gilbert, which is in Mingo County.)

When I was 17, I had a run-in with a Gilbert police officer, and it nearly got him shot. Officer Peck wasn't so much a bad guy as he was rigid—too rigid and demanding, I thought, toward his daughter. Of course, a 17-year-old knows better than anyone how others should behave. Officer Peck's teenage daughter was a good girl and a good student, but he wouldn't let her have any fun. He was very much a disciplinarian, made her walk the straight and narrow and hardly let her out of the house.

One day, I approached Peck and told him that he was being too hard on his daughter and that he should let her live a little bit and have some fun. He told me it was none of my business, but I persisted with my point of view. Next thing you know, we got into a pretty heated argument. At one point, he acted as if he was going to hit me, and I did the same to him. He even threatened to arrest me, but I didn't back down. No one stepped in to break us up, but I think each of us began to consider the consequences of our actions. We may have blinked at the same time. In any event, the anger subsided, and we cautiously parted ways.

I was on my way home when I came upon Mom, who was carrying a loaded .38-caliber pistol in her right hand. One of my friends had raced home with erroneous news of my trouble with the law, and she had come either to spring me from jail or to shoot Officer Peck between the eyes. It took some time for her to cool down and unload the pistol, which she did only after it was clear to her that no harm had come to me.

When we wanted to see a movie, we would have to go to Iaeger or Omar, either one about 17 miles away. We usually went to Omar, where the West Virginia Coal and Coke Company had a theater. In addition to watching a movie, we also hoped to find unattached, pretty teenage girls. I recall one night when I was 16, Roy Nester, Audrey Spratt, Pierce Fox and I went to Omar to see a movie. It must have been an uneventful trip. I know we didn't stumble upon any starry-eyed beauties looking to meet eager 16-year-old boys. On the way home, just on the other side of Stirrat, we decided to stop at the Golden Eagle beer joint, not to get a beer but to see if there were any young beauties inside. We went into the smoke-filled tavern and found our way to the back room, where we came upon a couple of girls interested in dancing. I danced with the two girls while my buddies cooled their heels.

I didn't know anyone there, so I started talking to Pierce, the likeable brother of the boy who years before had run me out of his family's new car. The jukebox abruptly stopped playing, and I noticed that two of my movie-going buddies were heading for the exit. Pierce said, "Buck, look behind you."

I turned and saw that several guys were closing in on us. We were standing against a wall, and I knew we were in trouble. I thought that they were going to beat the crap out of us, but I might get in one good lick before I was knocked senseless. I dropped the cigarette that I'd been smoking, allowing myself the freedom to swing at the nearest body.

This one guy said to me, "Don't you think it's time that you get your ass out of here?"

"Yep, I'm going," I answered, still planning to land a punch.

Boy, he must have read my mind because he hit me before I could hit him. Others joined in, and they about beat me to death: broke three of my ribs, broke my nose and hit me in face so hard that my eyes turned black and nearly swelled shut. One of them hit Pierce over the head with a beer bottle, but he was able to keep his feet and fend for himself. I, on the other hand, was knocked down to the floor, and they kicked me without restraint. The only thing that kept them from killing me was the beer joint's owner, Bob Hatfield, who came to my aid swinging a blackjack. If he hadn't beaten them back, I might've died right there. (Bob Hatfield, by the way, was the youngest son of Devil Anse Hatfield of Hatfield and McCoy fame.)

Talk about being sore. I hurt all over, particularly my ribs. In those days, you didn't head off to a hospital because you were hurt. You went home and nursed yourself back to health, and in this instance, it took a while to recover—and to extract a pound or two of revenge.

A couple of months later, I took a girl to the same movie theater at Omar, and as we were coming outside after the show, I spotted one of the fellows who had helped to beat me senseless. I told my date to wait for me as I began to walk down the wide steps that led from the theater. I had the tactical advantage of approaching my foe from above and behind. I tapped him on the shoulder, and as he turned, I hit him hard. He went tumbling down the steps, and I was right on him. I beat the crap out of him, and after a few moments, he just gave up the fight. I got off him and stood up. "Do you know who I am?"

"Oh yeah," he said, "I know who you are."

"Damn you," I said. "I should've killed you, the way you boys treated me."

My high school coach, Frank Hatfield, was quite a guy and, without a doubt, the toughest man I've ever met. He coached me in basketball, football and boxing, and he made a lasting impression on me. Frank had struggled to become a teacher because it had been difficult for him to find the money to make it through Concord College (now Concord University), so he boxed professionally to help pay his way, earning as much as $50 for a big fight and $35 for a typical match. Money like that went a long way back then, and Frank was eager to succeed.

I recall travelling with him on more than one occasion to Jenkins, Kentucky, where bouts took place regularly in front of crowds of up to 5,000. One of these fights I remember distinctly. Frank fought in the middleweight class against a boxer from Cincinnati, Ohio. I don't recall his opponent's name, but he was a black fellow and a skillful boxer, so good, in fact, that in the first six rounds this fellow just about beat Frank to death. I was in Frank's corner with another guy, and I tried to get Frank to give up. "Frank, let's quit," I implored. "Throw in the towel. Save it for another day."

"No, no," he replied, oblivious to my concern.

When the bell sounded for the seventh round, I feared a knockout was in the making. But, lo and behold, it was Frank who knocked out the other fighter! Where he got the power and focus to do that, I'll never know. But the knockout was clean and Frank was victorious. Unbelievable!

On the trip home, everyone in the car was quiet. As we were crossing into West Virginia, Frank, who was riding in the back seat, sat up and asked, "Who won?"

Frank was a decent, upstanding person. I never heard him say as much as "damn" in all the years I knew him. During high school, I was one of the few who knew that he and another teacher were secretly married, something that was forbidden in those days. He and his wife, Margaret, made a perfect pair. Each was devoted to the other, and both were dynamic members of our community. (Margaret was the sparkplug in putting together the first Gilbert High School

Reunion in 1980. She was the one who tracked down former teachers and students who had moved away from Gilbert, and she spent countless hours working with others to ensure that the reunion was a rousing success. Few people know how hard she worked, but she deserves a great deal of credit.)

I was almost the valedictorian of my high school graduating class, but I made my one and only B in chemistry and that knocked me out of the running. I suppose I could've made an A, but I didn't care for chemistry and didn't study much. The valedictorian was a young lady named Lena, a native of Hungary who lived with her uncle, keeping house and cooking for him. She was a very humble person, who had lived a very tough life to that point. She made all As and deserved the title. Lena later married a classmate, George Hontas, who became a teacher, and they moved to Ohio. Although she would have excelled, she never made it to college.

In my high school graduating class, there were 14 girls and five boys. About half of the kids who started high school dropped out before finishing. Times were so tough and many families were so strapped that they seized almost any opportunity for additional income. In most cases, it was the boys who dropped out and went to work. The girls had a little better chance to stay and get their diplomas. Of my graduating class, I believe that I'm the only one still living.

Willis Stinson, who graduated from Gilbert High School a few years ahead of me, became a good friend and mentor. We grew up in similar circumstances, and he struggled to make it through high school. After graduating, he attended college with the help of the local Ford dealer, Charley Peake. Willis pushed me to go on to college and suggested that I could pay my way by gaining a football scholarship at Marshall College (now Marshall University). I kept telling him that I didn't think I was good enough for a football scholarship and that I would be wasting my time, but he persisted. He took me to the Thundering Herd practice field in Huntington, where I got an abbreviated tryout. I ran a 40-yard sprint against the starting quarterback and beat him. I got to punt a few times and run a few plays.

Cam Henderson, who was both the school's football and basketball coach, talked to me afterwards and explained that he had already used up all of his scholarships but offered me free books and tuition if I wanted to play. I had to turn down his offer because I had no way to pay for room and board. I would have enjoyed going to college, but it was not to be. Some years later, an old friend told me that I was lucky not to have gone to college. Rather than the success I found in the business world, I might've ended up as a high school football coach in some forsaken little town.

After high school, I would often referee at football and basketball games. At that time, refereeing was a dangerous undertaking. The rivalries among small towns in southern West Virginia could be fierce, and it wasn't out of the ordinary to have bench-clearing brawls. Occasionally, whole stands of spectators would empty. Some teams were so eager to win that they would go to almost any extreme to do so. It was literally town against town, and sometimes the game would have to wait until the fighting subsided.

I was an umpire at a football game between Matewan and Burch, and Coach Rometta, the Gilbert High School football coach, was the referee. We'd already had a couple of fights in the first half, and as the second half began, a Burch player, whose team was being beaten badly, reached under his pant leg, pulled out a lead pipe and whacked an opposing player right over the head, setting off a horrendous fight.

A couple months later, at a basketball game between Matewan and Burch, I was paid triple, a whopping $15, because they couldn't find anyone who dared to referee the game after what had happened on the gridiron. At the beginning of the game, I got both teams together and read them the riot act, "Now, the first one of you who makes an illegal move, anything out of line, I'm going kick your ass off the floor and right out of the building, so you won't be able to even watch the game." I didn't have a bit of trouble with either team. I called more fouls than I should have, but I was not going to let that game get out of control.

I once played football for Burch High School when I was 25 years old. They referred to it as "bringing in a ringer." It happened more than once at more than one high school. Bringing in ringers was commonplace, especially in games with teams from out of state. I recall in my junior year of high school, we played a team from Grundy, Virginia. My coach played in that game, and we whipped the Grundy team.

In the game where I was a ringer, Burch was playing a team from Belfry, Kentucky, and I helped out at halfback. I was given time off from work, in fact, so I could practice with the team before the Saturday game. I played a pretty good game that day, even though Belfry won 15 to 12. After the game, everyone had to share the same shower facilities and a huge fight broke out—a big naked fight! I got well out of the way and watched as two football teams, probably 35 people altogether, everybody naked as a jay bird, duked it out in the shower. It was a scene that defies description.

After graduating from high school, I got into the restaurant business briefly, going into partnership with my former French teacher, Don King, who put up $100 to buy inventory yet continued to teach while we tested the waters. We were successful at first; perhaps I should say we were popular. He and I both lavished food and drink on the pretty young ladies who visited our establishment, and soon we had given away more than we earned and were forced to close.

In 1980, we had a high school reunion for the classes from 1926 to 1945. It turned out to be a big affair with 610 former students and spouses attending a banquet, and over 1,000, including their children and grandchildren, at a picnic the next day.

We tracked down Mr. King, who had earned a Ph.D. and was teaching at Southern Illinois University, and begged him to come to the reunion because we had a special reason for his attendance. In fact, I sent our plane to bring him to Gilbert. At the banquet, I presented him with a check for $3,800, repayment plus compounded interest for his ill-fated $100 investment in our restaurant.

The Gilbert High School reunions have been quite popular, so much so that we couldn't invite all classes at once because there was not enough space to seat all who would attend. In July 2010, we were able to invite classes through 1985, not because we increased capacity but because 162 alumni and teachers had passed away since the 2005 reunion. For the record, I was not the oldest attendee. That honor went to Elizabeth Sparks Vinciquerra from the class of 1935. Since Gilbert High School has played such an integral role in my life, I have set aside money, about $50,000, which will cover the cost of two reunions after I'm gone.

When I attended Gilbert High School, we played our football games on Betty Island on the Guyandotte River, but it was truly an island only when the water was up. In 1951, I bought a portion of Betty Island from the Depew family, built my first house and lived there until my wife, June, died.

In the late 1970s, the Mingo County Board of Education decided that Gilbert needed a new high school. The plan called for a college-sized gymnasium and an auditorium that would seat at least 400 people. During the early construction phase, the board decided that it could not build the gymnasium and auditorium as originally envisioned, and it began to consider ways to downsize and save money. Gilbert High School students, believing that they were being shortchanged, went on strike. The strike had been going on for several days, when I got a call from Jay Rockefeller, then West Virginia's governor, asking if there was anything I could do to get the kids back to school.

"Well," I responded, "if the board had done what it promised the people, there wouldn't have been a strike in the first place. Nevertheless, I'll see what I can do." I met with the board, and it became clear to me that there weren't sufficient funds to carry out the original design, so I told the members that, if they made the commitment to build the gymnasium the size as promised, then I would furnish the funds to build the auditorium. The board accepted my offer, and I donated $600,000 to build the auditorium. I did insist, however, that the auditorium be named in honor of a former principal, Lowell Phipps.**

The Class of 2011 was the last to graduate from Gilbert High School, and students from Gilbert are now attending the new Mingo Central High School. While it is sad to lose our alma mater, the new high school has better facilities and a broader curriculum, giving our young people even greater opportunities to excel.

Mingo Central High School was built on a former surface mine site, part of a strategic plan that includes the creation of the I-74 King Coal Highway and industrial site development, including a coal gasification project. All of this was spearheaded by the Mingo County Redevelopment Authority, and it proves that coal companies working with the community and government can play a truly creative role in enhancing the future after mining.

* When Miss Ridgeway first came to Gilbert, she was driving a brand-new Dodge coupe. The first place she stopped in town was Crago's garage because her poor automobile was steaming like it was about to blow up. The car was so hot that I couldn't even release the radiator cap. I said, "Ma'am, we'll have to wait a little bit to let it cool off before I can add any water. Do you have any idea what happened to cause this situation?"

"I don't know," she answered, "but it's been a long trip from Louisville."

With a little more prodding, I learned that she had driven the entire trip from Louisville in second gear. It's a wonder she completed the trip, even in a new car.

** Lowell Phipps was a gentleman I greatly admired. He was a teacher and later principal of Gilbert High School. He was both well read and witty, a real asset to the community. Later in life, he contracted multiple sclerosis, a debilitating disease that ultimately forced him into a wheelchair. Leaving the field of education, Lowell became an agent for the Jefferson Standard Life Insurance Company. In 1974, he was the number one sales person for Jefferson Standard for the entire country. Lowell had a positive attitude that was unsurpassed. If ever my spirits were down, I could visit him, and his fountain of optimism and good cheer would always brighten my mood.

Chapter Five

In 1939 I was still working at the garage in Gilbert. Crago had sold it by then, and Johnny Cline was my boss. On February 25th, Mr. Cline gave me a cash advance of $30, which amounted to a month's wages. I borrowed a car from Lee Ellis, Jr., and my high school sweetheart, June Montgomery, and I headed off to Kentucky to get married. June's basketball coach and teacher, Oma Lester, and her husband, Alex, went along with us as witnesses.

It was dark when we reached Stone, Kentucky, where we got Preacher Byrd out of bed to perform the ceremony. We sought out Preacher Byrd because he was well-known for marrying couples who eloped. (He also officiated at the marriage ceremony of Fred and Christine Shewey, two dear friends whom I write about later.) Preacher Byrd quickly put on a pair of pants and a shirt and married us in short order with his wife taking part in her nightgown. I handed him a $5 bill, thanked him for performing the ceremony at such a late hour and that was that. Off we drove to Gilbert to return the Lesters, then on to Logan to spend a two-night honeymoon at the Aracoma Hotel. When we came back to Gilbert, we moved in with Mom and Ras because we simply couldn't afford to live on our own.

June's dad was very upset that we had gotten married. Our icy relationship got even icier, and it took a long time to thaw.

June and I lived in two rooms in the old section of the house: a bedroom and a little kitchenette. June cooked on a two-burner coal stove, something she had never done before. She was used to eating meat regularly, but in our new household, we rarely did. After a time, she thought she might starve to death. One day she asked, "Buck, don't you ever eat meat around here?"

"No honey. We can't afford it."

June got used to a meatless diet and learned to cook on that coal stove, even though it was a chore. Larry was born in December, and that little baby cried for nine months. I felt so sorry for her since she would sometimes have to rock him all night. Of course, I was working, so the responsibility of caring for the baby fell to her.

I needed to find a higher-paying job in order to better support my young family, and I turned to my former high school football coach, Frank Hatfield, for assistance. He had quit his teaching job because of politics. In those days, all of the teaching jobs in the Mingo County school system were managed by politicians. Obviously, Frank had either supported the wrong candidate in the previous election or refused to pay a kickback for the privilege of keeping his job. In any event, he had gotten a job in nearby Red Jacket, working in the coal mines. I asked Frank if he might be able to help me get a job at Red Jacket, and he offered to let me ride with him to work so I could apply for a job. It took persistence. Every day, beginning at 5:00 a.m. sharp, for 13 consecutive work days, I'd ride with Frank to Red Jacket and go to see the mine superintendent, Fred Cook. Every day, I'd be waiting when Mr. Cook arrived at his office. When he'd come in, I'd say, "Mr. Cook, I really need a job. Have you got anything?"

"Nope, son," he'd answer, "got nothing."

On the 13th morning, the mine foreman was also waiting for Mr. Cook, and I had been waiting longer than the foreman. Mr. Cook hurried in, looked at me and said, "Hell's fire, are you here again?"

"Yes, Mr. Cook, I still want that job."

Mr. Cook motioned to the mine foreman, "Hire this damn boy! He's worrying me to death!"

(One of the first things I had to do upon being hired was to get a Social Security number, and I got one under the name Buck Ellis. It was later in life, when I was in business for myself, that my attorney advised me to go by the name of Harless, and it was then that I started using my birth name.)

I began to work in the mines, and it was very physical labor. At first, we cleared steel track from the worked-out sections, breaking the pieces loose and taking them to the new working section. Sometimes, there would be a big slate fall on the main line, and we would be called upon to clear up the mess. We used 16-pound sledge hammers to break up sizeable pieces of fallen rock. We kept beating that rock hour after hour, while the superintendent stood or sat nearby holding a light on us. Many a time I thought I wouldn't be able to make it through the day, and many a day I told myself that I wasn't going to take it anymore and that this would be my last day. But I always got up and went back. It was real tough; the inexperienced new hires did the hardest work in the mines.

One day while I was waiting for Frank to come out of the mine at the end of his shift, I decided to walk out to where they were loading railroad cars with coal, an activity that is referred to as "dumping." I wanted to see the progress the company was making on an upgrade to an automatic dumping system. I started talking to Mr. Blankenship, who had been dumping coal at Red Jacket for years and years, and he told me, "Buck, you know, I don't think I can handle this newfangled contraption here, and I believe I'm going to retire."

Mr. Blankenship's retirement talk was my cue to speak with Mr. Cook. Even though I had only been on the job for six months, I wanted to see if I might be able to get transferred to work with that new equipment. The next evening, I went to see the superintendent. "Mr. Cook," I said, "I understand Mr. Blankenship is not keen on learning that new equipment for dumping coal, and he's afraid he can't manage it. I'd like to have that job if I could."

"Oh boy, you haven't been here long enough." Mr. Cook always seemed exasperated with me. Lo and behold, about a month later, Mr. Blankenship retired, and Mr. Cook gave me the job. The automated equipment proved easy to handle, and I made the transition to dumping coal rather smoothly. I was so happy to get away from the back-breaking work.

I was impressed with the engineers who worked at Red Jacket. They were young fellows, and they always seemed to be having a good time. From what I could tell, they worked very little, and I said to myself, Boy, that's what I need to be doing. One day, I struck up a conversation with H.B. Turner, who was the assistant chief engineer, and told him that I'd like to put in an application for a job with the engineering department. He didn't sound very positive, saying that he already had several applications on file, but I asked him to take my name anyway.

About six months later, Mr. Turner offered me a job in the engineering department provided that I get the OK from Superintendent Cook. I got up the nerve to ask and went to his office after work. "Mr. Cook, could I speak with you?"

He barely looked up at me.

"I've got a wonderful opportunity, Mr. Cook. Mr. Turner tells me that I've got a job in engineering if you'll give me a transfer."

"You haven't had your current job for six months," Mr. Cook snarled, "and now you want something else. I'm not going to give you a transfer. Get your ass out of here."

I made a hasty exit before all thunder broke loose. I sure wanted that engineering job because I wanted to advance myself; I wanted better. About a week later, Mr. Cook walked out to where I was dumping coal and said, "Buck, I'll tell you what. I might as well give you this transfer because you won't be worth a damn around here otherwise."

I took the transfer paperwork to Mr. Turner on a Wednesday, and on Monday, I began a new job in engineering. I started out doing surveying work, back-sighting with the outside engineering crew, and in about six months, I was promoted to transitman. About eight months later, I got an inside job as a draftsman, even though I'd never done drafting work before. I was a quick learner, and in a short time, I became chief draftsman. Of course, this was during World War II when young men were being called in large numbers to serve their country.

I had already received two six-month deferments from military service on account of having two children. With so many of my friends heading off to the armed forces, however, I started to feel guilty and concluded that I would forego any more deferments. The local draft board informed me that I would be drafted in about a month. I turned in my notice at Red Jacket and set out to put my affairs in order before being shipped out, but the draft notice did not come as predicted.

Three months passed and no draft papers appeared. I went to the draft office in Matewan to discover the reason for the delay, and a draft board official told me that I had been given a permanent deferment because coal was so important to the war effort. I returned to Red Jacket and to my job in the engineering department.

John Maurice, the chief engineer at Red Jacket, became a good friend. When he had to visit other mining operations, he would have me drive him in the company station wagon because he didn't like to drive. On these trips, we'd talk about any topic, some subjects being personal in nature. He let me know that he did not care for some of my extracurricular activities, particularly my involvement with other girls, even though I was a married man. At Red Jacket, I lived at the clubhouse, a boarding house for single employees, during the work week and visited June on weekends, so I had ample opportunity to stray.

If Mr. Maurice scheduled a trip, I'd have a pretty good idea about what would be in store. During the first leg of a typical trip, he would not speak a word to me—not a word. His silence brought on a sense of guilt in me, but I wouldn't say anything either. Before the return trip, he would say to me, "Go through Justice on the way back." There was a bootleg joint there called Effie's Place, and I knew that he meant that we going to stop there. I'd pull in to Effie's Place, and we would sit at the bar.

"Give me a doubly," he'd tell the bartender, meaning a double. He'd drink the double, and then he'd ask for another doubly. After a couple of drinks, we'd get back in the car and drive away, and as soon as we'd round the first turn, he'd light into me verbally, telling me what a sorry specimen I was for messing around on my wife. He wouldn't let up until we made it back to Red Jacket, a difficult 45-minute ride for me. After he'd had his say, that was that, and the next day he would be a congenial fellow again.

Throughout my seven years at Red Jacket, I didn't own a car, but I had access to the station wagon assigned to the engineering department. I would take it to Matewan in the evenings and maybe go to a movie, or I would drive it home and go to Welch to see June on weekends. Not everyone in the engineering department was keen on me keeping a set of keys or using the car for personal reasons. One day, Roy Isom, the assistant chief engineer, told me to hand over my keys, but I refused. When I told our boss, John Kelly, about Mr. Isom's demand, he told me not to worry about it. I was able to keep my set of keys to the station wagon, which was really important to me, but I made a mortal enemy of Mr. Isom.

Red Jacket Consolidated Coal & Coke Company was owned by Ritter Lumber Company, one of the largest and oldest lumber companies in the East. Ritter had a lumber division and a coal division. At Red Jacket, we got a new general manager named Mr. Kirby, who was brought in from the lumber division. Of course, he was in very a difficult position because he knew absolutely nothing about coal. People would tell him things, and he was never sure if what they told him was valid or not.

His secretary was a woman named Ida, and she was an attractive woman. She and I became very good friends, and we spent a lot of time together in the evenings. I guess Mr. Kirby found out about our activities because one day he called me into his office. "I understand," he began, "that you don't like the food that's being served here at the clubhouse."

I thought the purpose of my office visit was to discuss my friendship with Ida, but Mr. Kirby threw me a curve asking about food complaints. I had once grumbled to others about having to eat so much liver, but I hadn't set out to have a mutiny. Still, the woman who prepared the food for us had worked in the lumber division and was a good friend of Mr. Kirby, and I allowed that she may have complained to him about my remark.

"If I said anything," I answered, "it was that I was growing tired of eating liver five days a week."

"Buck," he said, changing the subject, "I understand you've been doing things you shouldn't be doing."

"This isn't about food is it?"

"Buck, why don't you resign right now? Collect your belongings and don't come back."

I was stunned. When the general manager asks for your resignation, it's the same as being fired, so I went upstairs, gathered the few things that I had in my desk and hurried back downstairs. Ida came out of her office with a look of concern.

I said, "Well, I just got fired."

"You go back upstairs and wait," Ida said. "I want to talk to him."

I did as she requested and waited for about 30 minutes. Then Mr. Kirby called for me to come down to his office and closed the door gently after I entered.

"Buck," he said with resignation. "I think I was a little

hasty. I don't want you to resign, but I do want you to change your way of doing things." He paused and took a deep breath. "Now, you're a married man, and you shouldn't be running around with other women."

I said, "Well, I can't promise that I'll stop because I might break that promise, and you'll get upset with me and fire me all over again."

"OK," he responded, "Don't make a promise you can't keep. I was a little hasty. You go back to work, and forget that this happened. "

What I didn't realize was that Mr. Kirby was very much in love with Ida, and she apparently did not care for him to the extent that he cared for her. I discovered that Ida told him that if I went, she would go too, and he couldn't stand the thought of that. I got my job back, but Ida stopped seeing me.

I worked at Red Jacket until 1947, when I moved back to Gilbert to start in the lumber business, something I did because I didn't know any better. Two friends of mine, Fred Depew and Junior Dotson, invited me to run a little, rinky-dink sawmill that they owned for a one-third ownership interest in the mill. I was naive and had the desire to succeed, so I took them up on their offer. I suppose naiveté and desire compensated for good sense.

It was a one-man operation. I did all of the work and I labored many long hours day after day. In the beginning, I even did my own bookkeeping. There were times when I would get up at 1:00 or 2:00 a.m. to do paperwork, then go out and work at the mill from daylight to dark. Later, June assisted with the books, which helped a lot, but those first few years were tough.

My goal was to try to buy out my partners as soon as I could. By the end of the first year, I'd bought out Mr. Depew, who didn't expect much for his share of the operation. The second year, I worked extra hard to buy out Mr. Dotson, who had a tendency to show up on days when a check was due to arrive. If he got to the check before I could deposit it, I would never see the money. After buying out my partners, the mill was mine, what there was of it.

Mostly, what I remember from those early years in business was the work, the consistent struggle to survive and succeed. However, some memories from that era are sharp for completely different reasons. I recall one morning in 1953 or '54, I was heading into town at about 6:30 a.m. for a cup of coffee at the Guyan Restaurant before heading to the sawmill. I drove carefully that morning because it had snowed about six inches the night before, and the roads were slick. In fact, it was still snowing lightly. Behind the theater in Gilbert, I saw a big clump of something on the side of the road. As I drove closer, I recognized that it was a man in his tee shirt and boxer shorts, nearly covered in snow, and I pulled over to see if I could help.

It was Jake Mounts, the town drunk. He lay motionless, the freshly-fallen snow covering him. Beside him were his shoes and clothing folded in a pile. At first I thought he must be dead. Who could have survived a six-inch snowfall wearing hardly any clothing? When I got a better look, I saw that he was still alive because the snow was melting around his nostrils and mouth, and little bubbles kept forming along his lips as he breathed. Perhaps in a drunken stupor, he had decided that he'd made it home and had pulled off his clothes before he fell into what he thought was bed. I quickly drove to the restaurant, got my brother Fred, and together we collected Jake and his belongings from the roadway and took him home. All the time we were with him, he was out like a light.

Later in the morning, maybe about 11:00, I drove into Gilbert and saw him walking across the bridge in the center of town. I don't know if he took a break from the bottle that night, but I do know he survived his night in the snow.

Jake, who never had much money, was quite a character around town. His life was alcohol, and his goal was to buy cheap wine and get drunk as quickly and as often as he could. Another time, Jake was found lying along the roadway, and they took him to the undertaker, believing that he was dead. Russell Adams, the proprietor of Adams Funeral Home, put Jake's body on a slab and was preparing to embalm it when he heard this awful gurgling sound. The noise was so intense that it frightened Mr. Adams, who quickly determined that Jake was alive.

Jake moaned, "Where am I?"

"Buddy, you're in a funeral home about to be embalmed."

Jake sat up, said nothing, slowly got his bearings and left the funeral home to live another day.

It was over 10 years later before his tragic lifestyle got the best of him. One morning, he was found dead, fully clothed.

I once sold a carload of basswood lumber to Belcher Lumber Company in Bluefield. Belcher, in turn, shipped this lumber to its customer, Holt & Bugbee Company in Boston, Massachusetts. Later l got a call from a fellow at Belcher Lumber who said, "We received payment on that carload of basswood from our customer in Boston, but he's deducted $600 from the agreed upon price. He said the shipment was defective, and he wasn't not going to pay full price. So we're going to have to deduct $600 from the amount we promised you."

I was livid. "What do you mean defective? We sent perfectly good lumber, exactly what was specified." I stewed over the bad news for a while. Six hundred dollars was a whole lot of money back then, and I could not afford that kind of loss. I talked to my inspector, a competent older fellow who had checked the shipment before it was sent out, and he confirmed that the material we shipped was according to specification. I got the address for Holt & Bugbee, rounded up my gray-haired inspector, and together, we took a flight to Boston to get to the heart of the matter.

My 75-year-old traveling companion had never been on an airplane before and was quite fascinated with his first flight. He sat by the window and watched it all with great interest. We were flying at about 10,000 feet, but it became clear to me that he did not perceive just how high we were. "Well, my, my, what do you know?" he exclaimed, looking out the window, "Look at all of those little chickens down there!" I honestly don't know what he saw, but I know it wasn't chickens. Still, I didn't have the heart to tell him that he was mistaken. I have often wondered what he told his wife and family when he got back to Gilbert: "There we were way up in the air, and I looked down and saw all of these chickens!" Did his wife conclude that there were gangs of giant rampaging chickens somewhere between Gilbert and Boston?

We made it to the lumber yard in Boston, and I told the manager that we had shipped a railcar of lumber to his yard, about which there had been a serious complaint, and that we wanted to see things for ourselves. As soon as we approached the lumber in question, we recognized that it was not what we had shipped because it did not have my inspector's grade marks on it. "This isn't our lumber," I said.

"Well, that's what they sent to us," he answered.

We looked all over the yard for our lumber and eventually found our shipment. "Now, here's our lumber. We can prove it," and we did.

We left there in agreement with the yard's operators that our lumber had met and exceeded their specifications. I and my travelling buddy, who was having the time of his life, flew back to West Virginia. Upon our return, I telephoned the president of Belcher Lumber Company and explained that we had flown to Boston to investigate and had discovered what had really happened. I said, "I expect you to pay the full amount of this transaction, plus the cost of the airfare and other expenses incurred." Mr. Belcher was speechless for a time, but we eventually worked out things to my satisfaction.

Chapter Six

My son, Larry, was born on December 7, 1939, at home. His birth was assisted by Dr. Clark, who delivered hundreds, if not thousands, of babies around here. I came home from work and there he was: an energetic baby fresh to the world. I was happy and proud, but being just 19 years old, I was not ready for fatherhood. When you become a father at such a young age, you don't know what the hell is going on.

Larry was a good boy growing up; he never sassed me and always did what I asked him to do. He was an all-around good kid and a good student. After Larry finished the sixth grade, a recruiter from Greenbrier Military School asked me if he could speak with him. The recruiter invited him to Camp Shaw-Mi-Del-Eca, the school's summer camp along the Greenbrier River, and Larry decided to go. After he had been there for about three weeks, I got a call early one morning with the report that there had been an outbreak of spinal meningitis at the camp, that Larry wasn't sick, but that I should go get him and bring him home.

Once home, we talked about Greenbrier Military School, and he told me that he really wanted to go to school there. June was adamantly opposed to the idea of sending our son to a boarding school, and I had sincere reservations. But Larry wanted to go, so I enrolled him. When the time came,

June helped Larry pack up his clothes, and I drove him to Lewisburg to attend the fall semester. Along the way, Larry got very quiet, and I could tell he was troubled.

"Son, do you really want to go to school there?" I asked. He didn't answer. Perhaps he had already become homesick. "Look," I said, "it's OK, I can turn around right now."

He was silent for about a minute more before he said, "I want to go." Larry attended school there for five years, and it proved to be very good for him. It was a fine school, and he thrived there, excelling in both academics and sports, especially football.

One weekend, June and I visited Larry for Parade Day at the school. Late in the afternoon, he sat with us during one of the ceremonies. June studied him closely and exclaimed, "Larry, your ears are as dirty as they can be! What in the world?"

Our attention was diverted from Larry's dirty ears to the ceremony at hand, and we hardly noticed that he disappeared for several minutes. When he returned, his ears were as red as they could be: they were clean but as red as ripe strawberries.

When Larry graduated from Greenbrier Military School, he was a mature, self-confident young man.

Mom died in June 1944 at age 62, and she suffered a terrible death. Months earlier, she began complaining of abdominal pains and visited a doctor in Man who diagnosed her with ovarian cancer. Rather than surgically remove the cancer, he placed radium on the diseased tissue. That quack gave Mom a massive overdose of radiation, and she suffered horrific pain from that moment on. The radium caused her entire abdomen to become burned and disfigured with a reddish, distorted, cracked, hard-caked appearance. I can remember to this day her moaning and screaming from the devastating pain.

After the radium treatment, she went to see another doctor in Huntington. Dr. H. D. Hatfield was a former governor of West Virginia and a highly regarded physician. She spent about three days in his hospital before Dr. Hatfield concluded there was not anything that he could do for her. She came home and lay in bed her final months in unbelievable pain. Although her pain was so intense that it made her scream, I'm certain that what kept her focused on living was the anticipation of my daughter Judy's birth. Mom said to me more than once, "I want to live long enough to see that baby."

Judy was born on April 10th and Mom held on until June 6, 1944, the date many Americans remember as D-Day. That afternoon, I was standing out in the yard, listening to the momentous news on a battery-powered AM radio, when they called me into the house, saying in a tone of finality, "You'd better come in now," meaning that it was time to say our goodbyes.

She was conscious up to the moment she left this world, and all the time she was thinking of others. "Honey," she told me, "now I want you to be a good boy," just like she was talking to a kid. "You take good care of that little baby, and be a good father to your kids." Just before she died, she looked at me intently and said, "You're losing the best friend you ever had."

"Honey, I know that," I answered. "I know that."

She was gone five minutes later.

Ras was devastated.* I was devastated too, but I felt that I had to be strong to help pull the others through. Mom had been the leader of our household, and nothing was the same without her. To this day, words fail me when I think of her passing. She was the strongest and most compassionate person I've ever known. She was the best mom anyone could have hoped for, and I am a lucky fellow indeed.

Judy was born at Welch Hospital. I remember taking five-year-old Larry to see his rosy little sister for the first time. A friend later asked Larry about his new baby sister, and he exclaimed, "Oh, she's very red, but I'm sure it will wear off." For some unknown reason, he began to call her Rochester after a character played by Eddie Anderson on The Jack Benny Program. He called her that until she was 10 years old.

Judy was a good kid, and she never caused us any trouble growing up. Her grandmother Montgomery lived with us for a number of years, and she and Judy were very close. In fact, Judy slept with her grandmother throughout her childhood.

Judy loved horses so much that Morris Justice, my mechanic at the sawmill, gave her a pony. He somehow found one that had once worked in the coal mines, pulling loaded cars of coal at Kimberling Collieries. That pony had a lot of spunk in him, and he loved Judy. I can recall looking out the window and seeing Judy standing on the back of that pony while it ran at a full gallop. Whenever Larry would try to ride it, however, that pony would buck and kick and throw him off every time.

Judy adored Larry even though he would occasionally get her hot under the collar. I remember when they would go to see a movie at the little theater in Gilbert, June and I would give them a little extra spending money. Judy tended to save her money, and Larry almost always spent his. Judy generally had a few dollars saved while Larry was typically broke. Her brother would borrow money from her but never pay her back. She would complain about unpaid loans, yet turn right around and make another loan because she was so generous toward her big brother.

I recall the return trip from a family vacation to California in 1954. We were staying the night in a motel that had a pool. I lounged reading while Judy and Larry horsed around in the pool, which had two diving boards, one about six-feet high and the other perhaps 15 feet. Larry talked Judy into diving from the high board by promising that he would follow her and do the same. Judy climbed the ladder, walked to the diving board's front edge, took a moment to focus and sprung from the board as if she were an Olympian. Alas, Olympic-trained she was not, and she struck the water flat, slapping it hard with tender flesh. Goodness, it had to have hurt terribly. She came close to crying but did not.

Larry saw how badly the dive had stung her and showed no proclivity to make the lunge himself. I thought it only fair that he fulfill his promise, so I reminded him of his pledge. Being an obedient son, Larry climbed up to the high board and faced the water below, although he paused a good deal longer than Judy had. Larry's dive turned out to be very similar to Judy's, but when he hit the water, the crack was louder. Both children had confronted apprehension and fear and both suffered injury, albeit short lived. I think Larry came away with greater respect for his kid sister because she had not hesitated.

We lived on an island on the Guyandotte River just outside of Gilbert. There were only two houses on the island, a small one that a couple lived in and a larger house with our family.

Consequently, Judy had no one to play with nearby. One day, Judy sauntered into the house wearing a bathing suit, and her behavior was suspicious enough for me to undertake an investigation. I learned that she had slipped away from her mother, swum across the river, walked to the sawmill office, spent some time there and returned home by again swimming the river.

June and I bought Judy a piano when she was about 10, and she took right to it and played it regularly for a number of years. I was a member of the Kiwanis during her childhood, and she attended meetings with me and played the piano while the members sang. She also played piano for the high school chorus during class and for concerts under the direction of Miss Anne Phipps.

Judy attended public schools in Gilbert and was involved in many activities, including the band and cheerleading. She played the clarinet and saxophone in the high school band. Her band leader, Dana Dorsey, worked with her and helped develop her musical skills, and she became quite accomplished. She tried out twice for the State Band, an assemblage of the state's best high school band members, and was accepted each time.

We lived about a mile from the Gilbert schools, and when her mother didn't pick her up at the end of the school day, Judy would walk home. Often she'd stop at the office, which was on her way, and assist Junior Hatfield, our office manager, with different bookkeeping and office tasks. Junior was impressed with her ability to learn new things and was a willing teacher.

She was a very talented individual, and I was consistently proud of her and of her achievements.

Our truck drivers parked their rigs across the road from the office, and late one afternoon, one of our drivers and I were leaving the office at the same time, talking about nothing of importance. All of a sudden, I noticed one of our big trucks moving seemingly on its own toward the river. I set out running hoping to catch the truck, when the driver advised, "Don't worry, Buck. That's just Judy. She'll be alright." Not only had Judy found someone to teach her office skills but how to drive big trucks too!

"Does she do this regularly?" I demanded to know.

"I wouldn't say regularly, but pretty often," was his meek reply.

"Well, I want it stopped!" She was an adventurous young lady, and I wanted her to have the confidence to take on the world, but that frightened me.

During high school, she was invited to attend Girls State, a summer camp sponsored by the American Legion Auxiliary, where attendees learned about government and citizenship. Several of the kids talked Judy into running for attorney general and she was elected. She was proud to have won the election and appreciative of the opportunities provided by the Girls State program.

I remember January 23, 1955, very well. The day began as the lowest point in my life. Even though I was married to a devoted wife and mother and had two wonderful children, my personal life was in shambles. Throughout my married life, I had partied and womanized as if I was single. There came a point when I feared that I had wrecked my life and was about to lose my wife and children. I have never felt more alone or lost.

I don't know how I ended up at the Gilbert Presbyterian Church that Sunday night, and I don't know what the preacher preached or recall the songs that were sung. Perhaps you've heard of people who say God spoke to them. Well, I've never heard God say anything to me, but I can tell you this: something very good happened to me in church that evening. A sense of calm came over me, and I felt forgiven. And I experienced a feeling of redemption. Those moments in that little church changed my life. Afterwards, I told the minister, Norman Morgan, that I wanted to be baptized, and I told him why. I felt entirely different, just like a great load had been taken off my shoulders, and I knew that with the Lord's help, I was going to work through my problems. Later I talked to June, telling her how sorry I was and asked her if she would be baptized with me, and the next Sunday she, Judy and I were baptized. June realized that I was ready to change and she forgave me. This was a new beginning for me and for our marriage. I learned that being forgiven can be the one thing that can turn a man's life around.

From the day that I was baptized in 1955, I have been a member of the Gilbert Presbyterian Church, which was formed in 1897 with 12 charter members. Serving a small congregation over the years, it has survived through good times and bad, and it certainly means a lot to me.

Larry went to the University of Kentucky for a time and then to the University of Miami. While he performed well at both schools, he did not have a strong academic purpose, so he transferred to West Virginia University, where he studied more seriously and graduated with a degree in business. His goal was to study law, but during his senior year, he got married and his new wife was soon pregnant. He came home and said, "Daddy, I can't be a lawyer now. I've got to go to work." Larry started working with me at Gilbert Lumber Company.

Larry's new wife was the former Maureen Lockwood, the daughter of my accountant, Maurice Lockwood. Interestingly, neither Maurice nor I had any idea that our kids were even dating, much less planning to get married. Larry and Maureen made a fine pair. They moved to Gilbert and in a short time had two healthy boys, Jamey (James Howard) and M.K. (Maurice Kirk).

Larry took a load of responsibility off of me. In the beginning, he said, "Daddy, you've been getting up at 4:00 to 5:00 a.m. for years. I'll take the early shift and you can come in later." He worked hard, and he was a very good businessman who could read a person almost instantly. I relied upon him a great deal, and it was he who promoted the bold idea of doing business in South America. When we started transporting lumber from South America, he moved to Mobile, Alabama to manage the lumber yard there. Mobile became our distribution hub, where we shipped lumber to points throughout the world. During our working years together, I was always impressed with his talent and drive.

One day when Judy was 19, I got a call from June saying that Judy had disappeared.

"What do you mean disappeared?"

"She's gone. A lot of her clothes are missing and her car is gone too."

We discovered that Judy had run away to New Orleans in the little Austin-Healy that I had bought her when she graduated high school. We learned that she was staying with a cousin who lived in the Big Easy. She found a bookkeeping job at a local lumber yard and got romantically involved with a young man who was from there. June and I were worried sick about her, so we convinced Judy to return to Gilbert. I gave her new boyfriend a job helping the mechanic at the mill, but he was just a kid and didn't care much to get his hands dirty.

She and her young beau got married, even though they were far too young. It was clear to me that the marriage wasn't going to work. Her new husband, who was of Spanish ancestry, was obviously missing his friends and family. After about three months, I asked him, "Are you homesick for New Orleans?"

"Oh, yes, very much," he answered.

"Would you like to go back?"

"I sure would."

I had bought the newlyweds a new Oldsmobile as a wedding gift. "Why don't you take that Oldsmobile," I suggested, "and head on back to New Orleans?"

The next day he was gone and that was the end of the marriage, which had lasted just six months.

Judy later married Bruce Burgess, who had grown up in Logan, and they had two daughters, Stephanie and Beverly. Everyone thought they had a good marriage, and no one in the family recalls them ever having a cross word. One evening, however, they came to June and me and told us that they didn't love each other anymore and were going to divorce. That floored us.

At the time, Bruce was working for us as superintendent of a surface mine, and he offered to resign his position because of the divorce. My response was, "Absolutely not, Bruce. While circumstances may have changed, we have a great friendship and I want to maintain it, as well as our work relationship." We've remained good friends over the years. I have deep respect and affection for him, and I believe the feeling is mutual. Bruce is happily married to the former Debra Phipps, the daughter of my good friend Lowell Phipps, a principal of Gilbert High School. Bruce and Debra have two children, Blake and Megan.

After an amicable divorce, Judy and the two girls moved to Tennessee. Judy bought a farm outside of Shelbyville and raised Tennessee Walking Horses. At one time, she had the top breeding farm for Tennessee Walkers in the state. She now resides in Murfreesboro, Tennessee. Her daughter, Stephanie, attended Webb School, a private boarding school in Bell Buckle, Tennessee. After graduating from Webb, she attended West Virginia University. Her younger daughter, Beverly, attended Webb for a time and then transferred to public school where she graduated. Both of my granddaughters are smart and hardworking, and I'm very proud of them. Beverly resides in nearby Shelbyville and raises cattle, and Stephanie lives in Mobile.

Sadly, later in his life, Larry got hooked on whiskey, and it killed him, although it was a long, drawn-out affair. When he moved to Mobile in the early '80s, he'd drink occasionally. Over time he drank more and more. I'd try to talk to him about it. "Larry," I'd say, "you're an alcoholic."

"Now, daddy," he'd protest, "I'm not. I'm not."

"Son, it's obvious that you're an alcoholic and that you're doing yourself harm. You've got to quit." But he couldn't. I understand that it's nearly impossible for an alcoholic to admit that he has a problem and needs help, and Larry just couldn't reach that conclusion. Over time, he grew tired of the business and asked me to buy him out. I did, but I have often wondered if it was the right thing to do. He received several million dollars in the buyout and squandered a good part of it partying with friends all over the country.

His wife, Maureen, reached the end of her wits, and she told Larry that she was going to file for divorce and that he would have to leave. Larry simply left and didn't take anything with him. He never went back for any of his personal belongings or mementos. I know there were a lot of things in that house that he really wanted to have, but he would not return. He moved to Costa Rica, and he and Maureen divorced.

Near the end, he was in Costa Rica, and I got a call from his employee, Julio. "Mr. Harless, I'm scared to death about Larry." He spoke in broken English, but the concern in his voice was unmistakable. He said, "You know, he tried to kill me with a hatchet. He's going crazy." I made arrangements for a medical flight service to go to Costa Rica to get Larry and bring him back to the U.S. for treatment. There was a doctor and two nurses on board the airplane. I don't know how they got him on the plane, but I think they drugged him to a point that he became passive. When I first saw Larry on U.S. soil in Mobile, he was on a gurney being transferred from the plane to a waiting ambulance. He looked really bad, and he was quite surprised to see me and Fred Shewey, my dear friend and business associate.

"Daddy, what are you doing here?"

"Son, they told me you were sick."

"There's nothing wrong with me." He was so weak that he could hardly move and was shaking too.

I went to see one of Larry's friends who was a lawyer, hoping to find some way to keep Larry in the hospital, even if it was against his will. I asked Larry's friend point blank, "How long can we keep him in the hospital?"

"Against his will," he answered, "only 36 hours."

"Can I get a restraining order of some kind?"

"Oh yeah. But you understand that if I assist you in obtaining the order, Larry will never speak to me again?"

"I've got to do something. I'm fighting for his life. I've just got to."

"Buck," he said, "damn this is hard, but I'll help you do it." He went to a judge and got the order. A deputy sheriff stood outside Larry's hospital room for two weeks.

When Larry understood what had happened, he told me, "Daddy, I'll never forgive you for this."

I said, "You'll forgive me. When you get well and are feeling better, you'll forget this. You know that I did it for your own good."

Eventually he forgave me.

I was back in Gilbert when he left the hospital. He was still so weak that he could hardly walk. Nonetheless, he gathered up four or five of his buddies and headed for Las Vegas, Nevada. At that point, I gave up because I had no options left. It was clear to me that he would drink himself to death, and he got worse and worse in the following weeks. One night I got a call from Larry's older son Jamey. "Paw," he said, "you'd better come down here. Daddy's awful sick."

Without delay, I flew to Mobile and found Larry in terrible shape. He didn't even know me. My son died the next day. It was such a shame: he was so smart and he had so much going for him. Even the wealth he had so diligently earned was nearly gone. It was just so sad.

Hundreds of people gathered for his wake and funeral, and I've never seen so many flowers. It was a testament to how highly regarded he was and how much people liked him. Two individuals, both businessmen, approached me and told me essentially the same story. They said that, had it not been for Larry, they would be broke and that Larry's help and generosity had been key to their present-day success. It made me proud to hear those stories, yet it saddened me all the more that such a capable, warm-hearted person had been lost to alcohol. I learned from that awful experience that no matter how much you love your children, you can't help them unless they are willing to be helped.

June was a loyal wife and a dedicated mother. She was not very outgoing, and she wasn't one to put on airs. She was, however, a person who was very determined in her ideas, and it was difficult to change her mind once she had it made up. She made instant appraisals of people she met. For June, first impressions generally became lasting impressions. She did not like crowds, and for that reason, I often went places by myself. In fact, some people thought I wasn't married. It wasn't that I didn't want her to go with me; it was that she just didn't care for large congregations of people. As she got older, she became more that way.

June's mother, Emma, came to live with us in 1960 and stayed for 28 years. She and I never had a cross word, but I left the room on more than one occasion to ensure an unblemished record. She came to our home when June's dad's drinking became unbearable. He got so bad over time that June placed him in Huntington State Hospital, where he eventually died. When he wasn't drinking, he was a decent individual, but he just couldn't live free and not drink. It broke June's heart that she had to put him in a mental hospital, and it took a long time for her to get over the fact that he died there. I would say to her, "Honey, you had no choice."

June would go to Brazil with me, but that's different than being in a crowd. She'd go down and stay in the house we built at the mill, and she enjoyed that. We had a cook/housekeeper who couldn't speak any English, but she and June found ways to talk all day long. I often wondered how they did it, since June didn't speak a word of Portuguese and the housekeeper didn't speak a word of English. Somehow they found ways to understand each other. June enjoyed her trips to Brazil, and we sometimes stayed a month at a time.

I bought a helicopter that I used to get places quicker, and June told a story about it that went something like this: "I had a radio in the kitchen that Buck could contact me from the helicopter as he was flying. He'd call and say something like, 'I'm about 20 minutes out,' so I'd know when to start warming his dinner. I'd hear the helicopter approach from a distance, the sound getting louder and louder, and I knew that he was preparing to land in the front yard, where there was barely enough room because of the trees. He'd come in right over the house and onto the lawn. It was all very loud. Then he'd shut the engine down and come into the house like nothing had happened."

I can add one detail. We had a dog, a boxer, who was deathly afraid of that helicopter. It was June's primary responsibility to get that dog out of the yard before I landed.

June and I loved each other. She must have loved me because I got into a lot of things I shouldn't have as a married man, and she stuck with me even when I didn't treat her right. She forgave me and gave me a chance to hold onto my family. Our marriage lasted 60 years and three months when she passed away from problems associated with emphysema. She had smoked about all her life and paid a huge price for it. She was on oxygen for her last two years, yet she still wanted to smoke. We kept cigarettes from her mainly because I was afraid she might blow herself up in that oxygen-rich environment. She wanted a cigarette to the day she died. I look back now and think that I should have never denied her cigarettes. I'm so sorry I did.

My two grandsons have birthdays just days apart. M.K.'s birthday is on the 20th of September and Jamey's is on the 24th. When they were young, M.K., who was a year younger, would have his birthday party first, and Jamey would throw a fit. He'd tearfully announce to his parents, "I'm older! Why does M.K. get a party before me?"

As a child, Jamey was a tad wild. One day when he was about four, he was playing in his Batman costume. For some reason, he got angry at his mother and dove through a glass door, suffering life-threatening cuts over his body. Jamey nearly bled to death before they reached the hospital. Thank goodness, he's overcome his bad temper.

Neither of the boys went to college. Once, we rented out a ship that we owned for use in the movie The Ghost Ship. The producers painted the ship black and both boys made good money shuttling people and materials back and forth by boat. Jamey stayed in the charter business, and M.K. got into the lumber business, managing one of our retail operations in Savannah, Georgia. While he was in Savannah, M.K. got involved with drugs and alcohol, and Larry spent considerable time and money trying to help him, but June and I didn't know a thing about his problems at the time.

Some time after Larry's death, I called M.K. at the Savannah office. I could tell from the receptionist's tone of voice that something was wrong. "Mr. Harless," she said. "M.K.'s not here."

"Where is he?"

"I really don't know."

"When was the last time you saw him?"

"Almost a week ago."

"Well, when he shows up, you tell him to call me."

When M.K. finally called, I said, "Son, I want you to meet me in Mobile."

On that trip, I found out about all of the problems that M.K. had given his parents, and my meeting with him was very grim and difficult. I was determined to let him know that if he didn't straighten up, dire things were going happen, and he would be left in the cold. I was not going to stand for his destructive behavior. "If I see you lying along the road," I told him, "I won't pick you up. You are not my grandson anymore. I never dreamed I'd have a grandson who would turn out like you have." I kept at him in the same vein and I really raked him over the coals. "Your daddy spent a fortune on you trying to help. Well, I'm not going to spend a dime. You and I are finished. You go ahead and do whatever you're going to do, but you stay out of my life."

The next day, M.K. went to Alcoholics Anonymous. He attended meetings in the morning and evening, every day for a good while. He has not touched a beer or anything since. Of course, I couldn't have done what I said I would do, but I guess I scared him. In any event, it worked. He now has a big, happy family with four kids: Chelsea, Kitty, Chase and Hannah. He's doing great, and he and his wonderful wife, Paula, are very involved in their church.

Jamey worked with me on an exciting product that never completely came to fruition: a fully automatic shotgun. It's an interesting story. A woman who worked for me named Betty Coleman had a son-in-law who partnered with another fellow to perfect a fully automatic shotgun. They invited me to help finance their work and I did. They kept working on it but continued to have problems. One morning I woke up thinking about the project: the fact that I had sunk $700,000 into its development and that it still didn't work properly. I called Larry and said that I was ready to give up on this thing unless he could find a way to make it successful. Larry located two retired Florida highway patrolmen who were able to perfect the product within about six months.

We contracted with a South Korean manufacturer, who agreed to set up a production line and ensure a quality product at a cost of $1 million. The result is a quite a weapon: a 12-gauge shotgun that fires at the speed of a machine gun, 360 rounds a minute with either a seven-shot clip or a 20-shot drum. It is a very effective close-combat weapon.

Jamey took on the responsibility of travelling the world to sell the gun, primarily to military entities. He was somewhat successful, selling in small lots of less than one hundred but never the thousands that we had hoped.

Jamey was demonstrating the weapon before a group of officers in the Cambodian military, and the country's king heard of the demonstration and asked to see it. When he handled it, the king was very impressed and said he wanted the gun.

Jamey said, "Well, I'll order one for you and have it shipped."

"No, I want this gun," was the king's reply. So Jamey handed his one demonstration weapon over to the king.

The last sale that I recall was to a gentleman who appeared in our offices in Mobile. He presented identification showing that he was with the Central Intelligence Agency and made a cash purchase of 50 guns at $600 apiece. We gave up on the project when the U.S. military passed on the weapon.

Jamey splits his time between Costa Rica and Alabama. He and he wife, Sjon, have two kids, Tripp (James Howard, III) and Hope. Jamey makes a living running three charter fishing boats based in a little town named Flamingo Beach on the Pacific coast of Costa Rica. He's also half owner of a furniture store in Mobile.

About three months after Larry died, I was at a luncheon meeting at Port Amherst near Charleston. Among those present was Gary White, who was then president of the West Virginia Coal Association. After the meeting, Gary approached me and asked if I had considered hiring anyone to replace Larry.

"No, not really," I answered, "but I'll probably need to sooner or later." I was pleased that Gary entertained an interest in working with me, but it was about a month later before I called him and asked if we could get together and talk. We met, and within an hour, we had an agreement for him to take over as general manager of the company. It turned out to be an excellent decision for both of us. Gary is extremely intelligent and very capable, and he's skilled at dealing with people and very knowledgeable about the coal business. When he started, he knew very little about lumber but he learned quickly. After about three years with us, he became chief executive officer, and I became chairman. Our relationship has been excellent, and in a way, Gary has become the son that I lost.

We sold 75% of our coal operation to an investment group, and Gary moved to the new company as the president and CEO, while I became chairman of the board. The investment group proved to be made up of very fine and honorable people. The investment group later sold the entire company to James River Coal Company, a transaction that we believe is good for our employees and for us.

Gary's father is the Reverend Glenn White, pastor of Central United Baptist Church in Logan. He's the kind of pastor that every Christian would like to have. Not long ago, Gary's mother, Catherine, died, and her passing was difficult for the family. She was a very fine lady and the ideal pastor's wife, working beside Glenn all of these years.

---

* Ras lived for several years after Mom died. He married again and lived to the ripe old age of 86.

Chapter Seven

In 1949, John L. Lewis, head of the United Mine Workers of America, called for a work slowdown commonly referred to as the three-day strike. Lewis allowed miners to work only three days a week, which dramatically decreased coal output. The strike harmed me and my business because I had a number of mining customers, who purchased a variety of lumber products for their operations. Indeed, that strike hurt a lot of people.

The Appalachian Hardwood Manufacturers Association received an invitation from the U.S. Senate Select Committee on Small Business for an association member to testify about the coal strike and the hardships it created. Specifically, the committee sought to ascertain whether Lewis and the UMWA maintained a monopoly of workers in the coal industry. I was not a member of the association, but since I had been in business only two years and was suffering financially from the slowdown, I was asked to testify. I went to Washington, D.C., and appeared before the committee. I was given the opportunity to make a statement, which I had prepared in advance. I argued that the union was causing great economic harm with its work slowdown and cited several examples.

When it came time for questions from the committee, no one asked a thing, except for committee chairman U.S.

Senator John Sparkman of Alabama, who disdainfully posed a blistering series. After the hearing was adjourned, Thomas Kennedy, a vice president of the UMWA, approached me and asked how long I had been in business.

"Two years roughly," I answered.

"Well, if you keep up this kind of conversation," he said, referring to my testimony, "you won't be in business long because the union will not tolerate it." I took his threat seriously since the union wielded great power at the time.

Back in '56 or '57, just after I'd built my second mill in Gilbert, I was contacted by Mr. Johnson, who was the president of Lorado Mining on Buffalo Creek near Man. He called me at home one night, told me he had a problem and wanted to know if I would be interested in helping him solve it. He did not want me to come to his office, and he said, "I'll come to Gilbert to meet with you."

We met the next day, and Mr. Johnson explained that Lorado Mining had been purchasing wood products from a fellow named June Lambert. Evidently things weren't going well with the relationship, and Lorado wanted to sever ties with Mr. Lambert and find someone else who could effectively provide the products they needed. He asked if I would take on the job, and I readily agreed. Johnson said that there might be a problem as a result of the change. Even though Lambert had failed to meet expectations, his company claimed to be union and Lambert might cause trouble. I told him that we'd cross that bridge when we came to it, and sure enough, we had trouble, lots of it.

The first four or five days of providing products to Lorado went well. I contracted for mine posts to come from a supplier in Lincoln County, and I was delivering other materials like headers, cap boards, and wedges. Things proceeded smoothly.

During the second week, I got a call from June Lambert himself, who, in addition to owning a sawmill, was also a constable in Logan County and well connected in local Democratic politics, including law enforcement. "We've got seven of your truck drivers arrested," he said, revealing an obvious act of intimidation.

I went to Man and discovered that Lambert had talked deputy sheriffs and other cronies into putting pressure on me and that they had arrested all of the contractor's drivers on flimsy charges. It took a while, but I got them all bailed out of jail and back on the road, hauling mine posts.

Lo and behold the next day, the miners at Lorado came out on strike. The situation began to spiral out of control, but I wasn't about to let them whip me. We were still able to get our trucks up and down the highway, but we were met by menacing pickets when we attempted to deliver our materials to the mine site.

I'd have my truck driver take a load of material to Man, and I'd meet the truck there. Then I'd drive the truck up Buffalo Creek to the Lorado Mining site and drive across the picket line. The first day, I didn't have much trouble. I unloaded the truck by myself by hand. (This was before the introduction of fork lifts.) Unloading the truck was real work, especially 16-feet long 4X6-inch hardwood headers, which weighed about 150 pounds each. With the task completed, I headed down to the bottom of the hill where the pickets stood, blocking the bridge. I pulled up to face them and yelled, "I'm coming across the bridge, so you better move aside. I'd hate to put any of you in the creek." When I rolled across, they jumped out of the way, and I went home.

The next day at Man, I met the driver with another load of material and took the truck up to the site as before. When

I pulled up to the bridge, about 100 angry pickets stood waiting. A big, intimidating black fellow came up to the driver's side window and called me a m----- f------ s-- of a b----. I was quickly surrounded by a mob intent on doing me harm, and the moment was intense. In fact, that's the only time in my life that, if I'd had a gun, I might've killed somebody. I nudged the truck through the mass of bodies and, thankfully, everyone moved out of the way.

I headed up the hill and unloaded the truck, all the time knowing that I might have serious trouble with the pickets at the bridge. On the return trip, I decided to stop the truck several yards before the bridge. I climbed out of the cab and addressed the pickets, "Fellows, I don't want to hurt anyone, and I'm not going to get hurt either. But I'm coming across that bridge, and I'm coming in a hurry. If you're standing in the way, you're going to get run over. I'm just warning you."

I got back in the truck, revved the engine and took off, and everyone jumped out of the way. I was happy to make it home that evening and very relieved that no one had been hurt, yet I knew that things could turn very ugly if nothing was done to diffuse the situation.

It so happened that the Speaker of the West Virginia House of Delegates, William Flannery, lived in Man, and I asked a friend of mine, Lacy White, who was also from Man, to speak with Mr. Flannery about the situation. I waited and hoped for cooler heads in positions of power to find ways to prevent violence.

In the meantime, Mr. Johnson called me to his office and began the meeting by asking how I was getting along.

"I haven't delivered anything for a while," I said, "because I had a little trouble getting past striking miners who were blocking the bridge."

"Yeah, I heard about that," he responded, "and I don't believe I would've done what you did."

"I was just trying to do everything I could to fulfill our contract, short of getting killed."

He said, "Well, I expected trouble, so I have to live with the way things turned out. Of course, I don't know what's going to happen. The men say they are on strike because I gave you the contract."

A few minutes later, Mr. Johnson's secretary called and said that the mine committee was there and wanted to speak with him. Mr. Johnson told her to have them come in and told me to stay put. The committee of striking miners entered the room, and one of them said, "Mr. Johnson, we've decided that we want to go back to work, and we'd like to start on the night shift tonight."

Johnson said, "Good, I'm happy that you're coming back, but it's too late to go back to work today. You'll have to wait until the day shift tomorrow.

The president of the local almost pleaded with Mr. Johnson to let them go back that night but to no avail.

I was relieved that the strike had ended. I came to find out that John L. Lewis had intervened by sending a telegram to the local leadership, which stated that he was going to remove all officers from the local union if they weren't back to work by the night shift. His telegram was the reason that they were so anxious to get back to work. Even though they started to work the next day, I don't think Lewis removed anyone from his post. But he sure scared the local officers.

John L. Lewis was different from any other mine worker leader that we've had. When men were wrong under John L. Lewis, he did not uphold them. Today, regardless of how wrong or how ridiculous a complaint is, the union supports it. That's a big reason why I don't want to fool with the union.

That strike was a very harrowing time for me, and I consider myself lucky to have lived through it. I was able to keep that contract for as long as Lorado stayed in the mining business, but I also made sure to seek out additional customers beyond the coal industry.

In the early '50s, I got a $65,000 loan from the Small Business Administration, which I used to build a second mill in Gilbert. The loan agreement stipulated that I could not make a capital investment of more than $5,000 without SBA approval. Whenever I needed to make repairs or invest in new equipment, I had to seek authorization from the SBA, and its answer was consistently no. It reached a point where my equipment was wearing out, and I was facing ruin. Still, the SBA would not allow me to make new-equipment purchases over $5,000. Frustrated, I met with SBA officials in Richmond, Virginia, who would not change the terms of the loan. They suggested that I find a bank to pay off the SBA loan, and I came to the realization that a new lender would be my only hope for survival.

I set out to find a bank willing to retire the SBA loan and provide additional operating capital. I tried the local banks to no avail and cast my net wider and wider, looking for someone who understood my needs and who was willing to make a reasonable loan. I made an appointment with a Mr. Given, the president of the First Huntington National Bank in Huntington. After waiting an hour for him to return from lunch, I showed him financial statements to bolster my case. He reviewed the paperwork carefully, then looked at me over his reading glasses and said, "Son, you don't need $60,000. You need $160,000."

I expressed irritation with him. "Mr. Given, I didn't come here for advice. I came for money. If you don't have money to loan, please give me back my paperwork."

I tried other banks and they all turned me down. Late one Friday afternoon, I was in Huntington again and came upon the Twentieth Street Bank. Without much hope of finding success, I entered the bank and stated my reasons for being there. I was ushered into the office of its president, Bernard McGinnis, Jr., and I shared my dilemma with him. He looked over my paperwork and said, "Let me give this some thought, Mr. Harless, and I'll see what we can do." I left the bank with the impression that Mr. McGinnis had politely brushed me off. It was depressing, and I drove back to Gilbert forlorn and fearful that I would soon be out of business.

On Saturday night, I pitched a good drunk and got home quite late. Sunday morning, the phone rang about 9:00 a.m., and it was Mr. McGinnis. "Mr. Harless," he said, "I'd like to visit the sawmill that you told me about."

"Fine, Mr. McGinnis. When would you like to come?"

"Well, I'm in Gilbert now. In fact, I'm calling you from the Gulf filling station."

Oh, was I surprised! I quickly got up, washed my face with cold water and hurried to the only Gulf station in town. There stood Mr. McGinnis, and inside his car, was his family. I led them to the mill, and he spent about an hour looking things over and asking questions. Finally he said, "Can you come to the bank tomorrow to sign the necessary papers to get rid of the SBA?"

I was relieved and elated. His bank paid off the SBA loan and provided me with more operating capital. I learned later that Mr. McGinnis once had frustrating dealings with the SBA, and that may have played a role in my getting the financing. The fact is that he saved me from going under, and I was able to pay his loan back without difficulty.

Over the years, forest fires have been a big problem in southern West Virginia. Because the land is mostly wooded, a small fire can grow devastatingly large quite quickly. During the Great Depression, fires would break out and the fire warden would hire locals to fight them. Sometimes, the people who fought the fire were the ones who started it because they needed money so badly.

When I got into the lumber business, I worked to minimize the threat of forest fires. Much of the land in southern West Virginia is owned by large corporations, and we tried and tried to get them to participate in a fire prevention program to help preserve these fine hardwood forests. By and large these corporations were unresponsive to our requests.

In 1957, when Cecil Underwood was governor of West Virginia, I was a member of the West Virginia Forestry Association. Together, we came up with the idea of having a statewide meeting on forest fire prevention. I insisted that we invite the heads of all of the land-owning companies: U.S. Steel Corp., Western Pocahontas Land Corp., Norfolk Southern Corp., C&O Railroad and others. I further insisted that the meeting be held at The Greenbrier, believing that the CEOs of these companies might be willing to attend a meeting of this nature if it was held there. Although there was considerable opposition to my proposal, it nevertheless prevailed.

I appointed a committee of 30 people to work on the meeting project, and we had a planning session in Charleston. Bernard McGinnis, Jr. served as the committee finance chairman. I had difficulty remembering the names of the committee members, and Bernard told me that I had to do better to be effective. He said, "Look, I've never met any of these people, but I bet you, by the end of the meeting, I can stand at the door and tell you the name of every single person."

"I bet you can't."

At the meeting's conclusion, he proved me very wrong, showing that he knew everyone by first and last name. That episode pointed out a shortcoming in me, and I worked to improve myself. (Sadly, as I grow older, memory fails me more and more, and I can forget other things in addition to names.)

We held a big two-day meeting at The Greenbrier, and the heads of the land-owning corporations attended. Governor Underwood was there and was very involved in the entire event. We were successful in proving the need for these companies to get involved in fire prevention programs. Cecil Underwood's presence and involvement helped greatly. One outcome of that meeting was that U.S. Steel spent considerable time and money building fire trails throughout its forests, which made these areas readily accessible to fire fighters.

I'm happy to tell you that in recent years, forest fires in West Virginia have diminished considerably and are not the menace they once were. I believe that this change stems from our meeting in 1957.

In the 1950s, almost all of the coal mines in West Virginia and other coal-producing states were unionized. At the beginning of the decade, there were over 100,000 coal-mining jobs in the Mountain State. All of that changed, however, when the mining industry fully embraced the use of machines to mine coal. By 1954, mining employment dipped to 54,000. By 1960, total employment was less than 49,000. But the movement to mechanization was necessary if coal was to remain competitive with other forms of energy. Even John L. Lewis saw that the industry had to give way to machines, and he negotiated a labor contract that acknowledged that fact. He was able to trade health and welfare benefits in exchange for accepting the reality that many miners would lose their jobs, and that those jobs would never return to the coalfields.

In southern West Virginia, the number of unemployed miners grew substantially. People were leaving the state, looking elsewhere for jobs and prosperity. Late in the '50s, Frank Alara, my son Larry, Fred Shewey and I began talking over the idea of starting a church pew factory. People certainly needed jobs, and we were producing good hardwood lumber, so you would think that we had a good idea. We believed it would take about $350,000 to get it started.

In 1960, John F. Kennedy won the West Virginia Democratic Primary, a triumph that significantly helped him win the nomination and the presidency later that year. When he became president, Kennedy was very interested in helping with the unemployment problem in West Virginia. In 1961, Congress passed and President Kennedy signed into law the Area Redevelopment Act. As a result of that legislation, the Area Redevelopment Authority was created under the U.S. Department of Commerce to spur new business activity in areas of high unemployment, and President Kennedy chose my good friend, Frank Tsutras, to head the southern West Virginia field office located in Williamson.

Tsutras thought that the church pew factory was an excellent idea but suggested that we create something bigger to employ more people. After much discussion, we decided to seek funding to start a factory to build furniture parts for the furniture industry in North Carolina. We applied to the Area Redevelopment Authority for a $1 million grant to start the National Seating and Dimension Company. Shortly thereafter, the grant was approved and the money made available.

We bought property at Pigeon Creek in Mingo County and built a very nice factory with excellent equipment. Then we began training unemployed coal miners to become woodworkers, but it was no easy task. The goal in furniture making is to get a 60-to-65% yield from lumber to finished piece and we were getting only a 35% yield. We had real difficulty getting the workers to take their jobs seriously; they seemed to consider their training and jobs as some form of welfare program.

We were in operation for just six months when the workers formed a union. All the while, we were presenting to the government, our business backers, monthly financial statements showing that we were losing money. No matter what we tried, we continued to lose money. The government gave us a total of $450,000 in additional funds under the Workforce Retraining Program. Once the government's money was gone, we put our own money in the company to try to make it go, but it kept getting worse and worse. The workers were doing crazy things to hold up production, typical union filibustering and gamesmanship. Finally we told the government that we were almost broke and ready to give up.

I bluntly described our situation to the workers. "Boys, now listen. You need to straighten up and help us. You've got to get with the program because we're going to have to close this plant if you don't."

The president of their local spoke up, "Oh, you can't close this plant. The government won't let you and neither will the governor."

I said, "The governor has nothing to do with whether I close this plant or not."

"Oh, yes he does."

This was on Wednesday. On Friday, we paid everybody in full and locked the doors. That night at home, I got a call from Hulett Smith, who was then West Virginia's commerce commissioner. He said, "Buck, you can't close that plant."

"Yeah, that's what that union president told me, Hulett, but it's closed. Listen, I've worn myself out. I've tried everything I know to do but it's impossible. Now, damn it, if you want to run it, you come down here and run it, but I'm finished with it." It was a very distressing time. I had worked my butt off trying to build something that would be beneficial for the area, and all I got was grief and criticism.

After we closed the factory, *The Charleston Gazette* published a very detrimental article about me, which more than implied that I was a crook and that I had received money I shouldn't have. It was written by James Haught, who is currently the paper's editor. Everyone who mattered to me knew that I had taken a beating on that furniture plant, but Haught made me out to be a real lowlife. It was untrue and it stung.

I recall going to Bluefield to attend a Norfolk Southern annual party, and I saw Haught there. Boy, I wanted to whip him so badly. I tried to get him away from the crowd, so I could smack him a good one.

"Hey, James."

"What do you want?"

"I want to talk to you. Come outside with me, so we can have a private conversation." But he wouldn't go. In a hushed voice, so others couldn't overhear, I called him everything in the book, trying to get him angry enough to fight, but he wouldn't do it.

I rarely think of that evening or of Haught, yet I am consistently amazed at what newspapers and reporters can get away with. I've learned that people can say or write things about you that are untrue, and there's not much you can do about it.

One of my biggest breaks in the lumber business came from U.S. Steel Corporation, which had a mining complex at Gary in McDowell County. The company gave me a contract to supply wood products to that mining operation. Indeed, I was able to lease vast tracts of timber from U.S. Steel in southern West Virginia and western Virginia. I negotiated the contract and leases with Jack Caffery*, the chief engineer at U.S. Steel Gary Works.

John Schroeder, the superintendent for U.S. Steel at Lynch, Kentucky, presented me a similar deal. The offer required that I build a mill in Cumberland, Kentucky, but I didn't have the finances to do so. Of course, I went back to Twentieth Street Bank, and it was able to loan me about $300,000, its lending limit. But I needed $600,000 altogether. Bernard McGinnis told me to make a call to his father, Bernard McGinnis, Sr., and I did. The elder Mr. McGinnis had an office in downtown Huntington, and I went there and shared my problem with him. He listened carefully as I described the situation and then called out to his male secretary to bring him a note. Then and there he made me an uncollateralized personal loan for $300,000, as bold an act as I have ever seen in business. Many would have seen his loan as foolish, but he apparently had faith that I could repay it. With this new financing, I was able to build the new mill in Kentucky.

With help from the McGinnises**, I now had three mills and almost 300,000 acres of timber under lease, and I was able to pay off both notes with this very good U.S. Steel business.

One night in November 1965, my mill in Cumberland, Kentucky burned down. In January 1966, a compressor at the Gilbert mill exploded, causing a fire that the workers were unable to extinguish. I had some insurance on both properties but not enough to cover the entire losses. Georgia Pacific Corporation had approached me earlier about purchasing my operations, not so much for the mills as for the timber leases that I held from U.S. Steel Corporation. After the two fires, its offer to buy me out made a lot of sense, and I agreed to do so.

My attorney and friend, Brooks Lawson, flew with me in the company plane to Augusta, Georgia, to formalize the buyout agreement. I thought I had asked a pretty steep price, anticipating that it would be negotiated down, but they agreed to my asking price right away. I didn't receive cash; I got stock in Georgia Pacific instead, and I had to agree to not compete with them in the Appalachian territory for a period of 10 years.

It was late in the afternoon when we finished up with the negotiations, so we decided to spend the night in Knoxville, Tennessee, because Taplin Field near Man, where we planned to land upon our return, was a daylight-only operation. It had been a long, momentous day, but when it came time to do so, I could not sleep. In fact, I spent the night walking the streets of Knoxville, trying to put into context what I had just done and wondering if accepting Georgia Pacific stock rather than cash was a smart or a stupid thing to do. In addition, Georgia

Pacific's willingness to readily accept my asking price left me to question whether I had asked enough in the first place. At 6:00 a.m., I awoke Brooks and the pilot, who both thought that I had gotten up early, but the fact was that I had never been to sleep.

I was 47 when I sold out in 1966. I suppose I could've not worked another day. But I enjoy work and new opportunities, and the Georgia Pacific deal certainly provided for new opportunity. By the way, its stock price held up well over time.

When timber leases were due to be renewed, U.S. Steel and Georgia Pacific could not come to terms. By then, I had finished my 10-year non-compete agreement with Georgia Pacific and was able to lease back these same timberlands from Pocahontas Land Corporation, which had bought the property from U.S. Steel.

* Jack Caffery and I began a lifelong friendship. He has been a highly principled mentor, and I value his advice and insight. Living today in Welch with his wife Pat, Jack spends his time helping his fellow man.

** Later in life, I donated $1 million to Marshall University for the Bernard McGinnis Scholarship Fund. To date, some 250 students have benefited from the fund, and to this day I am enormously grateful to the McGinnis family for the trust they placed in me. Both father and son are deceased and Muriel, nicknamed "Moo," the widow of Bernard McGinnis, Jr. passed away in February 2009.

Chapter Eight

Throughout my life, I've been blessed to have a number of really good friends. I met Frank Alara when I was working at Red Jacket. His stonemason father was Italian and his mother was American born. Frank had a hard life growing up, but he had an engaging personality and the energy and discipline for hard work. His formal schooling ended after the eighth grade. His first job was that of call boy at the Williamson YMCA, and his duties were to wake up the residents every morning.

When we first met, he owned two Piper J-3 Cubs, very reliable, slow-flying, single engine, two-seat airplanes, and Frank offered flying lessons to wannabe pilots. In fact, he was once a civilian flight instructor contracted by the U.S. Army to teach primary flying skills to young military recruits. Frank's flying exploits went all the way back to 1929, and his pilot's license was number 149 or some similar low number.

He built his first airplane. He bought the wooden airframe and his mother helped him cover the frame with cloth. I don't recall the full story, but he crashed on his maiden flight. He turned right around and built another one, and the second one he flew successfully. At one time, he barnstormed throughout the region, visiting county fairs and the like, where he took passengers on brief flights for a small fee.

He taught me to fly an airplane at the dirt-strip Nolan

Airport in 1943. It was a very good deal for me: he didn't charge for the lessons, and we used his airplanes and fuel. I soloed after six hours of instruction, flying a triangle from Nolan to Charleston via Huntington. When I got to Charleston, I decided to make the return trip to Nolan via Ashland, Kentucky. I was gone a lot longer than I should have, and when I landed at Nolan, Frank stormed up to the plane and yelled, "Where the hell have you been?"

"I decided to fly to Ashland before coming back to Nolan."

"I ought to kick your ass!" he exclaimed. Frank could get hot headed.

Frank always maintained parachutes for each of his planes. I was constantly after him to let me jump from a plane and parachute to earth. One day he grew impatient with my interest in parachuting. "Buck," he cautioned me, "shut up about this jumping business! That damn parachute hasn't been unfolded in 10 years, and I don't know if it will open or not."

I decided it would be wise for me to bite my lip. I learned from Frank that sometimes you just need to shut up.

Frank called me one day at work and said that he had just sold one of his airplanes, and he wanted to know if I would fly it to Knoxville, Tennessee, along with his mechanic, Happy, who would fly Frank's other plane and bring me home. I got permission to take some time off and got ready to fly to Knoxville. I went down to the airstrip at Nolan and there sat the two planes. "Is everything ready?" I asked.

"Oh, yeah," Happy answered, "everything's ready to go."

Moments later, we took off from Nolan and flew together after we leveled off at about 4,000 feet. Near Hazard, Kentucky, which is pretty rugged terrain, my engine started to spit and sputter. It wasn't cold enough for me to add carburetor heat, but I added some anyway. The sputtering subsided.

All of a sudden the engine stopped, and the propeller pointed straight up and down. It quickly dawned upon me that I was out of fuel. Our planes had no radios, so I was completely on my own. Frank had always told me that in a situation like this to always seek out and follow a river: if there was to be any land flat enough to land a stricken airplane, it would be along a river. I began a glide from 4,000 feet, looking for a river and flat land. The fallback to my primary plan was to land the airplane in the river and swim for it, so I had at least two options that afforded me the chance to live through this.

On the glide down, I spied a river and did just as Frank had trained me, lining up on the river and maintaining my glide path. At a couple hundred feet of altitude, I could see that the river made a sweeping left turn. At that moment, I calculated that I could make the turn but would probably have to dump the airplane into the river. I gently banked left anticipating cold water, when, low and behold, right in front of me sat a grass air strip with a small plane parked off to the side. Amazed at my good fortune, I made a near perfect dead-stick landing.

Happy landed a couple of minutes later and ran up to me. "Buck," he exclaimed in wide-eyed seriousness, "you landed downwind!" Proper landing technique requires that the aircraft be headed into the wind.

Exasperated, I said, "Happy, I had to land anyway I could because I didn't have any power."

We bought fuel at the airstrip and made an uneventful trip to Knoxville and back. That day I learned that you can land a plane downwind, but I don't recommend it!

Frank was once in the theater business and did very well. His first movie house was at Matewan, and the second was at

Delbarton. At Jenkins, Kentucky, he had an outdoor theater, and he also built one at Proctorville, Ohio. He hated television, by the way, because its burgeoning popularity was tough on theaters.

When he was getting the drive-in at Proctorville up and running, he spent a lot of time away from home, which tested the patience of his wife "Mat" (Madeline), who herself was quite a character. One night he got home late and didn't have a key to get in the house. He knocked rather loudly hoping to wake his wife. Mat, figuring it could only be Frank at this hour, quietly walked to the locked door, and in a conspiratorial voice, said, "Come on in. Frank's not here."

Frank worked very hard, and his efforts made him quite successful, even at a young age. When he was just 19, he was superintendent of a coal mine at Rawl, a small town near Matewan. Being 19 made him one of the youngest mine superintendents in the country. Later in life, Frank became president of the Bank of Matewan, and he was a very active member of the Methodist church in town. While he was treasurer of the church and president of the bank, he occasionally blended those responsibilities. If you made a pledge to the church and didn't pay it, he would take the pledged amount out of your bank account. He was so well liked that he got away with doing things like that.

One evening I stopped in a pharmacy at Matewan and ran into Frank, who had just become the father of a baby boy. "Frank, I understand there's a new baby at your house."

"Yep," he answered in all seriousness, "but there won't be anymore babies."

"Well, I'm surprised to hear that, Frank," I answered, knowing that he and Mat were elated to have children.

"No," he deadpanned, "Mat and I have found out what's causing it."

Frank was a true friend, who savored his Italian heritage. It is commonly claimed that Italian men love women. If that's correct, then Frank was clearly a true Italian because he loved pretty girls and had a habit of pinching women on the butt. I don't think he ever was unfaithful, but he certainly liked to flirt.

Each year the opening of the swimming pool at the Sprigg Country Club was a big affair with women wearing nice evening gowns and men in tuxedos. At one particular opening, Frank, who loved to play, and another jokester named Lefty Hamilton were having an especially good time flirting with this pretty young woman. At one point, the three of them walked over to the swimming pool. Frank turned to the girl and said, "Let's walk across the pool."

"Can you do that?" asked the girl, somewhat unsure as to the meaning of his offer.

"Certainly," Frank answered, full of confidence and charm. "Let me show you how." Frank and Lefty, with the girl in hand, entered the pool walking down the steps at the shallow end. Of course, with each step the water rose higher up their formal attire.

"No, no!" cried the girl. "I'm getting wet!"

"Wet, hell!" Frank intoned seriously, marching onward to ever deeper water. "Young lady, you have lost faith and are sinking all three of us!"

Frank's wife took his humor in stride. She watched the whole thing and said afterwards, "Well, I see that you've made an ass of yourself again."

Frank would sometimes go with a group to watch the Cincinnati Reds play baseball, and I recall one time four of us made the trip to Cincinnati to take in a game. On the way back, we decided to take a rest stop at a store along the highway. Frank headed into the store at the same time this young fellow walked out, and they bumped into each other. The young guy threw a fit, telling the old man—Frank was 60 by that time—to watch where he's going.

Most men his age might have offered a meek apology, but not Frank. "You little bastard!" he sneered. "Just who in the hell do you think you are? You get out my way!" Frank's anger was obvious, and the surprised young fellow reviewed his options and slithered away. Throughout his life, Frank had a temper that had to be reckoned with.

I was one of the founding members of a social organization that met at Sprigg Country Club. We called it the Mountain Club, and we gathered once a month for dinner and drinks. When we'd get together, we'd generally have a good time. I recall one evening after dinner, Frank was having an animated conversation with this fellow across the room. I could tell that the exchange was not going well, so I nonchalantly made my way over to where they faced each other.

Frank grew more heated and agitated. "You're a lying son of a bitch," Frank exclaimed passionately, and as if having one epiphany after the other, he yelled, "No, you are a double son of a bitch! No, you're a revolving son of a bitch! Anyway I turn you, you're a son of a bitch!" Frank reared back to hit the fellow, but

I interceded grabbing him from behind before he let go with a big right hand.

I learned that Frank had gotten mad because this fellow had said something disparaging about me. Rather than tell me what the guy had said and letting me fend for myself, Frank instantly took it upon himself to defend my honor. A true friend will do that for you.

Frank and his wife had four boys and one girl. He would tell people: I have four boys and each boy has a sister. How many children do I have? Some people would conclude that he had eight children.

Late in life, Frank came to me and said, "Buck, I'm losing my damn mind."

"What do you mean, Frank?"

"Well, I got up this morning, showered, shaved, dressed and took off for Williamson. Got down there, got out of the car and had no idea why I had come to town. I still don't know. I went home and asked Mat, 'Why did I go to Williamson?' She said, 'How in the hell do I know?' Buck, I think I'm losing my mind."

"Oh, you are not," I protested.

I look back now and see that incident as the beginning of his demise. Frank's mother had suffered a slow decline and spent years bedridden. She wasn't in a coma, but she lost her connection to the present and didn't know anybody for about 10 years. Frank was fearful that the same fate would befall him, and true to his fears, it did. He lay in bed for years, unable to communicate with anyone and died at home, a lonely death. Frank was quite a character and a dear friend.

I first met Fred Shewey in Kermit at a fundraiser that he hosted for Cecil Underwood in 1956. Fred and I hit it off right away because we had so many similarities, including having been married by the same preacher, although he was married a few years before June and I. Fred was in the oil and gas business when we first met, and beyond becoming friends, I bought a few shares in his wells.

Fred and I have a singular relationship. He will do anything in the world for me, and I will do anything in the world for him. We have been best friends through thick and thin, and I am blessed that our paths crossed many years ago. No one could ask for a more loyal friend than Fred, and we've had wonderful times together.

We love to tease Fred, and believe it not, he loves to be teased.

We opened a coal mine called Jumacris, named for my wife, June; Frank's wife, Mat; and Fred's wife, Christine. We had a number of meetings to get the mine up and running. At one meeting, Frank and I decided to pull one on Fred.

"Fred," I began quite seriously, "we all know that every winter you and Christine go to Florida and stay until spring. Well, that's got to stop."

"Stop?" Fred was incredulous. "Why do we have to stop?"

"Well, if you had attended all the meetings, you'd already know," Frank admonished.

"What meetings?" Fred was downright confused.

"Where we made the commitment to buy B&L Furniture," I said. Fred loathed the owners of B&L Furniture.

"We're buying B&L Furniture?" he asked. It was obvious to both Frank and me that Fred had clearly swallowed the bait.

"Already bought it," I answered, "and you're going to have to manage it because the both of us are too busy doing other things. Now, we know you don't care for the present owners, but the good news is that they'll be working for you. Of course, the bad news is that you won't be spending winters in Florida."

Fred looked intently at both Frank and me, still unable to fathom the news. "Going to buy B&L Furniture?" he asked again.

"Already bought it and you get to run it."

"Well," Fred concluded, "if that's what needs to be done, then I'll do it."

We let Fred believe our story for awhile. He even told Christine that there would be no Florida vacation that year. It was still incredible to him that we were going into the retail furniture business, and he was more than relieved when we told him that we had been pulling his leg.

Larry, Frank, Fred and I were playing golf one day at The Greenbrier. Even though neither of us is a gambler, Fred and I played for $50 a hole that day and on many other occasions. (Fred is the only person that I've gambled with.) Most of the time we played even, but on this day, he was beating me badly. Coming to the 18th hole, I was down $400. We both hit pretty good drives fairly close together, but for the second shot, he had to hit first because his ball was farther from the hole. While he was preparing to hit the ball, I walked up and placed two $100 bills on the ground, one on each side of his ball.

"Get out of here, Buck," Fred complained. "Get away."

I started chanting, "Hit the ball, Fred. Hit the ball."

"Get away from me! Get that money out of here!"

"Hit the ball, Fred. Hit the ball."

Fred took a swing completely out of rhythm, and his ball shot out at almost a 90-degree angle from its intended trajectory. I won the hole, and since we were playing double or nothing, we walked off the 18th green even for the day once again.

In 1973, Larry called one day from Mobile suggesting that we take a rafting trip down the Colorado River, and I thought it was a wonderful idea. We made reservations for a group that included Frank, Fred, Winston Cline, Larry, June and I. We flew west and landed at a dirt strip called Lee's Landing, right below the Hoover Dam. We spent the night at a motel there, and the next day, along with two friends of Larry's who had flown in from Memphis, Tennessee, we began a rafting trip down the mighty Colorado. It was a most interesting and enjoyable outing.

We had two young guides on our raft, and the trip lasted five days. We'd set up camp each night along the river. There was no need for tents because there was little chance of rain; we slept on blankets placed on the sand. Our guides were really good cooks, and they'd prepare hotcakes and bacon or sausage in the morning, a light meal for lunch and a luscious steak for dinner along with fried potatoes and all the goodies that go with steak. We camped under the stars: bright, uncountable stars in the blackness of night. The sounds were so pure and natural in those late-night and early-morning hours. Other than the occasional chirps of crickets and the soft rumble of the river, there was quiet.

I believe it was the second night of the trip, after we had finished dinner, when Fred, who had had a few drinks and was very talkative, decided that he was going to go fishing. The rest of us agreed that this was a good idea because we had grown tired of his chatter. Fred stationed himself at the river's edge, fishing pole in hand, and continued jawing about this and that as he fished. I very carefully sneaked up behind him, waited for the best moment to pounce and gave him a big shove into the river. Fred came flailing out of the water, drenched from head to toe, yelling, "Why did you do that, Buck?"

"I want you to shut up. You're talking too much and aggravating everybody to death!"

On the third day of the trip, we came upon a large, ominous rapid. As we approached, one of the guides said, "This is the rapid that Bobby Kennedy jumped in and swam through." As we entered the rapid, Larry and one of his Memphis friends jumped into the churning, fast moving, icy water, obviously seeking to match the Kennedy stunt. Through the huge, roaring rapid we went, and then through a second rapid. Everyone on the raft was concerned for the swimmers' safety, as we watched their heads bobbing in and out of the water. When we were finally able to pull them back into the raft, they were blue from the cold and beaten up by the experience. They were lucky to have survived.

Toward the end of the trip, Fred turned to me and asked, "How are we going to get out of this canyon?" The canyon was formidable with a vertical rock face many feet high, jutting up from both sides of the river.

"A helicopter is going to fly in to get us," I answered.

"I don't see how they're going to take us out of here in a helicopter," he responded. "How can a helicopter get down here?"

"I don't know, Fred, but that's what they said."

We beached the raft about noon, and when we got out, I noticed a small ledge near the base of the canyon. I figured the ledge was just big enough to land a small helicopter. "Look over there," I said to Fred, "I bet that ledge is where we'll get on the copter."

Fred did not care to fly in normal circumstances even on large aircraft, and he was petrified to think that he would have to ride in a small helicopter from that tiny ledge. "If I have to do that," he announced, "then I have to be drunk. Real drunk!" And very drunk he became. "Buck," he said, "I also have to go first, and you have to go with me."

"OK, Fred. I'll go with you and we'll go first." He had become fairly wobbly by that time, so he had prepared well. Together we got on the helicopter, and the pilot skillfully lifted us to the top of the canyon and to a gentle landing.

"Whoopee, whoopee!" cried Fred, elated to have made the trip. "Whoopee!" He staggered to the edge to look over the side.

"Fred, get your butt back here!" I yelled, fearing that he might slip and fall. Thankfully he staggered away from the edge.

We had an insurance company in Bermuda, and we used to go down there every three months for board meetings. We would often play golf, and during one trip, we played 27 holes in one day. Fred hadn't been keen on playing the last nine holes. "Man, I'm tired," he told us, but he played on anyway.

As we were finishing up, he lifted his golf bag to remove it from the cart and fell straight backwards. There he lay on the ground with his golf clubs and bag on top of him. "Fred" we asked, "what happened?" We were laughing, yet at the same time, we were concerned that he was OK.

"Damn!" Fred exclaimed, his voice rising, "I told you that I was worn out!"

We all laughed, including Fred, because it was such a silly moment.

We were once in the Cayman Islands for a coal meeting. One evening Fred became quite magnanimous and offered to buy dinner at a fancy restaurant for all of the attendees, about 25 people altogether. After we were seated and ordered our meals, Fred came over to me discreetly and whispered, "Buck, come outside for a minute. I need to talk to you."

We stepped away from the group. "Buck, I need to borrow $500," Fred said.

"Why do you need $500?"

"I don't have enough cash to pay the bill."

I laughed and said, "Gee, Fred. That's your problem. You're the one who offered to buy dinner. I'm not going to pay for the meals; you said you were going to pick up the tab."

"Hell, Buck, it'll be embarrassing for me to have to ask everyone to pay his own bill."

"That's your problem, Fred. You created this situation, not me."

He spied the coal company sales manager headed for the restroom and followed him inside, where he posed the question, "Do you like your job?"

"Sure," the man answered, "I love my job."

"Then give me your credit card."

Our company had never issued Fred a credit card, and after some harping from Fred, we got him one. Soon after, we were in Parkersburg at Benson International, one of our manufacturing concerns, hosting a dinner for all of the supervisory personnel. When we were seated, Fred asked me if he could use his new credit card to pay for the meal, and I said sure.

Without Fred's knowledge, Gary White, International Industries' president, sneaked over to our waitress and hatched a plan to play a trick on Fred. We had a good meal and good conversation. The waitress, who had done an excellent job for us, presented the check to Fred, and he gave her his new credit card. Moments later she came back, and in the most diplomatic way, she told Fred that there was a problem with his card. For some reason, it was not being accepted.

"It can't be," Fred replied. "I just got this card and activated it myself."

"I'll try again," she offered. She was gone for a time, and when she returned, she had bad news, "I called the company. They refuse to honor your card. Do you have another form of payment? Cash, in this instance, would be very appropriate."

"Hell, no," Fred answered, "not this much cash!" Fred could not believe what he was hearing, and the few of us in on the joke could hardly contain ourselves.

"Here, young lady, take my card," I said, handing the waitress my credit card. Fred was relieved and grateful that I had helped him out. For a long time, he had no idea that we had pulled one on him.

While it may seem that all we did was play jokes on Fred, the fact is that everybody loves him and holds him in the highest regard. He's such a joy to be around.

Fred and his wife, Christine, had a very happy marriage that lasted 69 years before she died. I've been with Fred and

Christine in a variety of situations all over the world, and in all of the time that I've known them, I've never heard a cross word from either of them. Fred misses Christine very much. She was a real sweetheart. Brooks Lawson always said to him, "Fred, you married up." I'm sure Fred would agree.

Fred has always pushed me into the limelight and worked to ensure that I received the accolades, while he was content to stay in the background. It didn't worry him whether he got a pat on the back or not. Yet he is deserving of many honors in his own right, and I can truly say that I could not have had a better friend than Fred.

Brooks Lawson served as my attorney for a number of years, and he guided me through a number of significant events and issues in my life. Were it not for his skills, of which there were many, I might have screwed up more times than I care to count.

Brooks came to Williamson in 1929, right after he graduated from law school at West Virginia University. He was a handsome man, an immaculate dresser, and he grew to become a highly respected attorney. He was a very loyal and good friend.

When he was a child growing up in Randolph County, he worked at a family-owned sawmill, which had a steam boiler that furnished the mill's power. One day when he was 16, he was working there, and a small fire broke out. He raced out on the deck and tried to extinguish it with a rather large fire hose. The pressurized hose somehow got loose from his grasp, and in his zeal to regain control of it, he badly burned his ankle. Even though he was wounded, he was still able to contain and extinguish the fire. In the aftermath, he sat thinking and decided that he would never work another day in his life. That's why, he said, he became a lawyer.

He was an excellent attorney and handled all kinds of work that one would expect to see in a small town. He even did criminal work, and people who got into bad trouble, like being charged for shooting or killing someone, would want Brooks to defend them. I once sat in on the closing arguments of a murder case that he was defending. His client, a woman, had caught her husband with another woman, and she had killed him on the spot. There was no disputing that she shot him dead. When Brooks gave his closing summation, tears just rolled down his cheeks. Consider this poor old widow, he told the jury. She was the one who raised the kids. Her husband hadn't helped at all. He just went on and on about how she had suffered indignity after indignity as the tears continued to stream. He obviously swayed the jury because they let her go free.

Brooks and his wife became pillars of the community, and they raised three fine children: a son who practiced law with his dad; a son who became an ophthalmologist; and a strikingly beautiful daughter who was queen of the 1955 Fourth of July Festival sponsored by the Kiwanis Club in Gilbert.

One day I received a call from then West Virginia University President Gordon Gee. "Buck," he said, "I'm going to Washington, D.C., to have lunch with U.S. Supreme Court Chief Justice Warren Burger." President Gee had once clerked for Chief Justice Burger, and they remained friends. "Anyway," he continued, "would you like to come along and have lunch with the chief justice and me?"

"Certainly I would."

I hung up the phone, excited at the opportunity, and in a few minutes, I called President Gee back with a request. "You know, my personal attorney and good friend, Brooks Lawson, would love to meet the chief justice. May I bring Brooks along?"

"Of course!" President Gee readily agreed.

A few days later, we flew to Washington and headed straight to the Supreme Court, where we were met by a Mr. Cannon, who gave us a tour around the court. After a time, we came upon a silver-haired gentleman, who was putting on his jacket; it was the chief justice himself. "I'll take over from here, Mr. Cannon." Chief Justice Burger continued the behind-the-scenes tour. At one point, we came upon the area where the Justices hear oral arguments. A spittoon sat alongside each of the nine chairs.

"Chief Justice Burger," I asked in mock seriousness, "I can understand how some of the male justices might wish to have a chew or a rub, but does Justice Sandra Day O'Connor?"

"Goodness, no." he laughed, "In fact, none of them do. Those spittoons have been here long before the current court."

We had an interesting lunch with Burger, who spent much of the time quizzing us on our opinions of events and news of the day. After lunch, he lit a cigar, as did my friend Brooks, who as a lawyer was completely mesmerized by the surroundings and the chance to "hold court," if you will, with Warren Burger. Soon Mr. Cannon reappeared and reminded the chief justice of an appointment at the White House. "Mr. Cannon," Burger said, as he prepared to leave, "please see that my car is available to take these gentlemen to the airport." It had been a fascinating two hours for me—and certainly for Brooks—and I was so pleased that Brooks got to come along.

In his later years, Brooks would call me and say, "Well, Buck, I just wanted to talk to the only friend I've got left." It was an exaggeration of course, but he just wanted to talk.

One time, he came to Gilbert for a social event at the church, and when he left for home, he got disoriented and headed down the highway in the wrong direction. A little later, he came back to the church and found Ruth Phipps, who was my secretary at the time. He told her, "Ruth, I've got a problem. I was driving up the road, but I didn't know where I was." She made sure that he left for home in the right direction.

A week later, he went to bed and stayed there. I'd go to visit him and he'd be in bed. We'd talk about everything and everybody because he wanted to know what was going on, particularly with politics—he was really into politics. I'd say, "Brooks, why don't you get dressed, and we'll just drive around, maybe go down to Chattaroy and get us a bite to eat." But he wouldn't do it. He stayed in that bed almost a year and was close to 80 when he finally passed away.

Old age can be cruel, and I can understand why people give up. You get worn out and you just don't have the energy. I think about it myself sometimes. Then I say, "Hey, quit thinking like that. Get your ass out of bed and go do some work."

Everett Thompson was an extremely fine person, who became a dear friend. He owned Buick and GMC dealerships in Kentucky, about a mile from Williamson. He was a solid person of high moral character and a businessman of impeccable integrity. Everett was an active member of the Williamson Presbyterian Church and served there as an elder. He and I never had a business relationship; we were just good friends.

I remember when a group of us were playing golf at a course in North Carolina. Everett was partnered with a gentleman who shall remain unnamed and Fred Shewey and I were paired as their opponents. Everett's partner tended to break the rules whenever his wished: moving his ball out of rough or slyly changing his lie. Sometimes he cheated boldly. Once he hit a drive that clearly landed deep in some scruffy brush, but when he struck his next shot, he did so from the edge of the fairway.

Everett approached me as we were walking to the green. "Buck," he said, "I'm going to call it a day. I just don't want to play with this guy. He cheats!"

"Oh Everett, we know he's cheating. Keep on playing, and we won't worry about it. We'll just make sure to never play with him again."

Everett played on, but Fred and I could see how he loathed a cheater. Honor and integrity were everything to Everett.

Eight of us were staying at the Grand Hotel outside of Mobile for golf and relaxation. One evening, we drove to nearby Pensacola, Florida, for dinner at a nice restaurant, and we were served by a very friendly and chatty young woman of Chinese ethnicity. The cute young lady provided excellent service and was particularly attentive to Brooks Lawson, something that Everett commented upon at the meal.

On the trip back, Everett continued to kid Brooks about the waitress. After a time, Brooks lost his patience. "Everett," Brooks asked, "don't you recall what Chief Justice John Marshall once said?"

"No, what did he say?"

"Everyone should spend a considerable amount of time minding his own damn business."

Occasionally my name would find its way into a newspaper story, and Everett would cut out the article and send it to me with a little handwritten note, reminding me not to get a big head because my name was in the paper. Invariably, he would close by writing, "Buck, I love you." It's unusual for one man to tell another that he loves him, but I learned from Everett that it's OK to do so.

One morning he went to his dealership and did little more than pour himself a cup of coffee before he sat down in a chair and died of a heart attack. I gave the eulogy at his funeral and related some of the funny experiences that we had shared over the years. I did not dwell on sadness because Everett would not have wanted that. Still, it was a difficult thing to do because he was an outstanding person and a dear friend. I miss him a great deal.

By 1953, I had built my second mill on Gilbert Creek right below the Horsepen Bridge, about five miles below the Gay Mining Company operation, which had been started a few years earlier by Harry S. Gay, Jr. of Logan. A fellow named Lawson Hamilton had a contract to auger coal for Gay Mining Company and was having a difficult time making a go of it.

Lawson often told a story about those hard times: Each day he would leave the mine with the clear intent of not returning the following day, believing that his contract was a lost cause.

Everyday he would pass my mill on his way to and from work and see me loading trucks, rolling logs on the skidway and otherwise working from daylight to dark. More than once he told himself, "If that damn fellow can make it, I can make it too." He'd go back the next day committed to trying once more. Eventually he succeeded with the Gay contract and over time became a very successful coal operator.

When Lawson was working in the Gilbert area, he rented a room above Joe Wayne Hatfield's restaurant, and on weekends, he'd return to Charleston. Lawson is the only transient that I'm aware of who became president of the Gilbert Kiwanis Club, and he was president for two years straight. Lawson loved to sing and perform. During his tenure as president, he talked us into presenting a minstrel show, and he directed the whole endeavor. Much to my amazement, he'd take individuals who I thought wouldn't be able to even speak on stage and have them perform solos—and perform them well! The show we put on was celebrated in the community, thanks to Lawson's tireless efforts and unbounded optimism. It was so highly regarded that people in Man invited us to put on a performance there and we did.

Anyone familiar with Lawson Hamilton knew that he lived life to the fullest. He loved people, and he loved to entertain and was happiest when he knew his guests were having a good time. Lawson was one of the most outstanding individuals I've ever known. Beginning with his time in Gilbert, Lawson and I became very close and enjoyed each other's company on many occasions.

He was an excellent singer, and he took advantage of any opportunity to perform, whether it was at a party, a ball game or at church. He and his son, Tripp, were choir members in the Old Stone Presbyterian Church in Lewisburg. Lawson loved the

Kanawha River about as much as he liked to sing, and he was a big supporter of the Sternwheel Regatta, which was held for years in Charleston around Labor Day. One year, the Regatta leadership asked Lawson if he would loan his helicopter to fly a large American flag over the Kanawha while a band played *The Star Spangled Banner*. Lawson knew his helicopter was too small to safely fly the flag, so he recommended a company from Toledo, Ohio, which he believed could do the job. The Toledo company wanted several thousand dollars to make the flight, and the Regatta committee balked at the price. Lawson offered to pay for the helicopter rental provided the committee let him sing *The Star Spangled Banner*. The committee agreed and he sang—with gusto.

Over the many years of my business life, I've had the good fortune to meet some wonderful people and make lasting friendships. Charlie Jones is one of those people. When I met him, his family owned Amherst Coal Company at Buffalo Creek in Logan County. At that time, it was the largest independent coal operation in the state. During my early days of sawmilling, I sold them a variety of wood products for use inside the mines and became good friends with Charlie and his brother, Herbert.

Shortly after my second wife, Hallie, and I were married, I got a call from Lawson and Charlie, saying they wanted to give us a party in celebration of our marriage. The party was to be held on the Momma Jean and the Laura J, sternwheelers owned by Lawson and Charlie respectively. Their plan was to have an evening cruise on the Kanawha River in the Charleston area. I'm not sure how many invitations were sent out, but both the Momma Jean and the Laura J were filled with people, and we enjoyed a superb evening on our river cruise. Of course there was a band, and Lawson sang *What a Wonderful World*, the standard made famous by Louis Armstrong. As we passed the University of Charleston, the sky lit up with a spectacular fireworks display, which went on for several minutes. The last fireworks displayed were bright white letters that read "Congratulations, Hallie and Buck."

Lawson died in November of 2007 at the ripe age of 84. I was honored by his family to give the eulogy at his funeral. This was difficult to carry out, but I kept my remarks as humorous as possible because he would not have cared for expressions of sadness and grief. I tried to convey Lawson's big heart and his love for people. We lost a fine fellow, whose shoes cannot be filled. He helped many people in trouble and started many people in business. All along he gave back in numerous ways as we are supposed to do. He is sorely missed by his many friends and associates.

Gilbert was incorporated in 1918, and it had 240 people living there at the time. That number is a little misleading because in the surrounding area that treated Gilbert as the trading center, there was a population of 1,000. Today the population of Gilbert is about 600, yet in the surrounding area there are 10,000 residents.

For the longest time, Gilbert didn't have a bank. Merchants and individuals had to do their banking with the Bank of Iaeger, Matewan National or a couple of banks in Williamson. In 1974, a local group put together $600,000 and founded Gilbert Bank and Trust. To help get it off the ground, a number of individuals made sizeable deposits; confidence grew quickly and Gilbert

Bank and Trust became quite successful. The new bank provided excellent service to its customers, who didn't have to drive elsewhere to bank, and of course, the money stayed in town.

Our bank even acquired many customers from other cities and towns in southern West Virginia. One of those was Richard "Dick" Preservati, who was in construction and coal mining. I got to know him when we considered doing a joint venture on some U.S. Steel property that we were able to lease. Dick wanted to use a lot of his used equipment and I wanted to buy all new equipment. I decided to give up my interest and Dick took over the whole thing and struggled with it for a number of years.

I was chairman of the board of Gilbert Bank and Trust, and Dick came to me seeking to borrow money to help strengthen his business. Dick was a hard worker just like his father and was trying mightily to make his business successful, so I leaned toward making the loan. Carl Lambert, the bank president, focused on the risk and was against making the loan of $450,000. By a majority vote of the board of directors, Dick got his loan. Unfortunately, he had difficulty making his payments on time. At board meetings, Carl made a point of telling us that Dick was behind on his payments. This went on for several months and became a little tiresome.

At one board meeting, after Carl again raised the subject, I asked him to tell me the payoff amount of Dick's loan.

"I'll get those figures for you tomorrow," Carl responded.

"No, get those figures for me now."

Carl went downstairs to retrieve the information and returned in a matter of minutes. I wrote the bank a check for the balance of the note and took over the loan and collateral myself. Afterwards, I thought what I had done was unwise, but I stuck with it.

Dick paid on the note, a little bit here and a little bit there. He came to me one day and said that he had paid off everybody but me.

"When are you going to pay me?" I asked.

"Soon," he answered.

In about three months, Dick returned and asked, "How much do I owe you?" The debt amounted to $555,657.92. Of that $187,401.48 was interest. Dick, as he usually does, tried to bargain. "Buck," he asked, "will you strike off the interest?"

"Dick, I could strike off your head! I made this loan knowing that it was risky and that it was going to take you some time to pay it off. I'm glad that you made it through and succeeded, but I'm not going to forgive the interest."

From that day on, Dick and I have been close friends and we laugh about his request for interest forgiveness. Hallie and I occasionally spend enjoyable time with him and his wife, Karen. He's doing well and is semi-retired. Recently he sold his company for $450 million, so he did OK.

At a coal meeting in Hawaii in 1979, I met a young man named Terry Dotson, who worked for Worldwide Equipment Corp., one of the largest Mack truck dealerships in the country. When we got back, I talked with him about taking over the Meade Chevrolet dealership in Gilbert, but he was far more interested in truck sales. We let the subject rest, and over time, we bought a number of trucks from Terry and Worldwide. I was always impressed by his manner and skills.

In 1984, a major stockholder of Worldwide Equipment lost a sizeable amount of money when a bank in Tennessee failed, and Worldwide was offered for sale. Terry asked me if I might be interested in purchasing the company, and I said yes. We purchased Worldwide and chose Terry to run it.

Benson Trailer Manufacturing, located in Mineral Wells, also became available, and I suggested we buy it too, so that we could offer both trucks and trailers. Terry had to be sold on the idea, but he came around. He served as president of both companies before they were split and operated separately.

When we purchased Worldwide, it had five locations throughout eastern Kentucky and southern West Virginia, and it has grown to 33 locations under Terry's leadership. We sold Worldwide Equipment Corp. to Terry and his employees, who formed an Employee Stock Ownership Plan (ESOP). They are doing exceptionally well.

When we purchased Worldwide Equipment Corp, an attorney named Bart Brown represented both Worldwide as the seller and us as the purchaser, which is unusual. But he did a fine job for both parties. He has become a close friend and advisor and has helped me with a number of projects. Bart is a true friend, and I'm deeply indebted to him for his involvement in my business affairs.

In all of my years in business, I've had only four secretaries, all of whom have been very capable, reliable and loyal.

Betty Coleman started in the early '50s. She, like me, was a high school graduate, and she came to the job without all of the prerequisite skills. She was a quick study, however, and became very effective at her job. She worked hard, was very dedicated and served me well.

My second secretary was Retha Cline. While she provided good service, she worked only a couple of years for me.

Ruth Phipps was with me for over 15 years. She was also very efficient and very loyal.

Sharon Murphy has been with me for the past 30 years, and during that time, she has become my right arm. She even seems to know what I think. She has access to my bank account and pays my bills. She is known among my business associates as one of the most personable people they know. She can handle difficult situations for me too, and she keeps people who she senses are not in my best interest away from me, even though we maintain an open-door policy, seeking to be as accessible as possible. In our small community, there are several requests for loans and gifts, and Sharon has learned how and whom I prefer to help, and she manages the giving very effectively.

It would be very difficult for me to function properly without Sharon in the office next to me. I'm deeply indebted to her for her devoted service all these years. I have asked that, when I'm gone, she continue to manage the day-to-day affairs of International Industries, Inc., which, after the sale of most of its assets, is a holding company with some real estate assets.

My mother, Bessie Brown Harless and
my father, Pearly J. Harless.

Rosa Brown Ellis, my aunt who became Mom.

George Erastis Ellis, whom everyone called Ras.

Brown family reunion, ca. 1930s.

Top and Center: Gilbert Grade School class photos.
Bottom: Gilbert High School.

School photos at age eight and 12.

Top: An early view of the Gilbert Presbyterian Church.
Bottom: The Gilbert of my youth.

Top and Center: Crago's Garage and wrecker.
Bottom: George Crago in later years.

Top: Gilbert High football team, 1934.
Bottom: High school graduation, June 1937.

Top Left: Our young family with June's mother.
Top Right: June in the early 1960s. Bottom: June and I celebrating our 60th wedding anniversary.

Top: Larry at Greenbrier Military Academy.
Bottom: Larry and Maureen in better times.

From Top: Judy with her pet chicken.
Before a school dance. As a high school graduate.

Top: With (L to R) Judy, Larry and June in the 1980s.
Bottom: With brothers (L to R) Fred, Frank and Milton.

Top: Frank Alara.
Bottom: Mat and Frank Alara.

Top: Fred Shewey showing off a great pair of legs.
Bottom: Christine and Fred Shewey.

Top: Brooks Lawson. Bottom (L to R) Gov. Cecil Underwood, Gary White and Randy Cline.

Top: Rafting the Colorado River. Bottom: The helicopter that carried us safely out of the canyon.

Top: First Gilbert sawmill and lumber yard.
Bottom: Ras Ellis (standing on the fork lift)
working at the Gilbert sawmill.

Top: Appearing with Gov. Cecil Underwood, ca. late 1950s.
Bottom: With Baron aircraft, ca. early 1960s.

Top: Mahogany logs.
Bottom: Sawmill in Brazil.

Top: Overseeing ship loading.
Bottom: Buck Miller at the Brazil sawmill.

Top: Forester Hayes Hamric beside a strikingly large black walnut. Bottom: Taking a break from a managers' meeting in Mobile, Alabama in 1990.

Top: Conferring with (L to R) Garland Brewer and Bruce Burgess. Bottom: The former lumber division's management and forestry staff.

Top: Receiving an honorary doctorate
at Marshall University, ca. 1980s.
Bottom: Commencement at West Virginia University, 1981.

Top: With (L to R) Lew McManus and Lawson Hamilton at the University of Charleston, ca. 1990s.
Bottom: An honorary doctorate from Concord College, which gained university status in 2004.

Top: With former WVU football coach Don Nehlen and Lawson Hamilton. Bottom: With Senator Robert C. Byrd.

Top: With (L to R) Spike Maynard, Gen. Doc Fogelsong, President George W. Bush. Bottom: Touring the new health center with Judie Charlton, MD; WVU President James Clements; John Brick, MD; and James Brick, MD.

With most of my family in 2009.

With Hallie at a dinner in Charleston.

With (L to R) SSgt. Margaret Akers, General Robert H. "Doc" Fogelsong and TSgt. Steve Collins.

Top: The WVU Marching Band performing before the inaugural Mingo Central High School football game.
(Photo courtesy of Chris Southard/CDS Images)
Bottom: Talking with players at the stadium dedication.

Working in my office, while Dusty catches a nap.

Chapter Nine

It was Larry who proposed going into the lumber business in South America, although his idea seemed a bit farfetched at first. He had a friend of Cuban heritage who assisted us in South America by translating and helping to navigate local business practices. Although he was Spanish speaking, he was able to manage Portuguese, the language of Brazil, the country where we ended up doing our greatest amount of business. In that era, the government of Brazil was not very friendly to foreign business interests. Beginning in 1964, the country was governed by its military, and the generals weren't enthusiastic about those who sought to export its natural resources. When we first went there, the economy was a mess and the government appeared incompetent. Nevertheless, we were fortunate to learn the ways of business in Brazil and were able to make a go of it even though we faced hardship and occasional catastrophe.

To kind of get my feet wet, I made two trips to Brazil, one with June and one by myself. I learned that, even far from home, it is undeniably a small world. During the first trip, June and I added Rio de Janeiro to the itinerary and stayed at the Copacabana Hotel. On Saturday evening, I asked the concierge if there was an English-speaking church nearby, and he told us that there was a Presbyterian church a block away.

The next morning, June and I attended services at the church. We went early and enjoyed coffee on a patio within the church compound. While I was sitting there, someone slapped me on the back and asked, "Buck, what in the world are you doing here?" It was the civil engineer who had helped build the water system in Gilbert when I was mayor.

After church services, we had lunch with him and his wife and learned that he had contracted with the Brazilian government and was advising them on how to improve their water systems. He lived in a palatial apartment along Copacabana Beach in Rio and was doing quite well for himself.

When I returned to the U.S., I told Larry that I thought we should build a mill in Brazil. However, he and his friend had already found a mill to buy in Ecuador, so we made the trip to Ecuador to investigate a little "peckerwood" sawmill in San Lorenzo, located at what seemed to be the end of the world. We bought the mill without much research or deliberation, and it turned out to be a mistake.

We spent a week during that visit and stayed in a little house that had a water tank perched on top of a small tower; we took cold showers standing underneath the water tank. I've never seen rats anywhere like those we found there. They were big ones, 14- to 16-inches long, and you could hear them running around all night long.

Fred Shewey and Larry were with me on that trip, and Fred would not eat any of the local food. He'd brought a suitcase full of Nabs with him, and the only things he ate and drank were those peanut butter crackers and beer. Larry and I ate in a restaurant that had a latrine along the back wall. The latrine reeked, and so did the restaurant.

One evening while we were taking turns having a shower, I heard Fred yell to Larry asking if he had any hair cream.

"I don't think so, but look in my shaving kit," Larry answered.

Moments later, Fred appeared freshly dressed with his hair slicked down in a way we had never seen before. Fred, we discovered, had inadvertently used toothpaste for hair cream.

We operated the mill at San Lorenzo, but it was difficult. At one point, we were loading a ship with products and needed more lumber to make a full shipment. We'd heard that there was another mill with excess lumber further up the river and made the 30-mile trip to see if we could buy some of it. Our mode of transportation was a dugout canoe, literally a log hollowed out in the form of a canoe, with a five-horsepower motor mounted on the back.

The mill's owner had lumber to sell and we bought it. He was a friendly black fellow, and he gave us a tour of his operation. Along the fringes of the camp, we noticed a number of native women wearing nothing but grass skirts. I had a camera with me and raised it to take a picture.

"Do not take a picture," the sawmill owner warned me sternly. "They do not take kindly to cameras."

I put the camera down not wanting to offend anyone in any way. (Later I learned that we were just five miles from a spot where headhunters had killed some Catholic missionaries years earlier.) Difficulties mounted and we gave up on the sawmill in Ecuador and set our sights on Brazil once more.

During my second trip to Brazil, I made an expedition into the jungle to investigate the timber potential. I slept in a hammock for seven nights, bone tired from each day's brutal hike. I vividly recall my first night in the hammock. It was just at the edge of darkness when I heard an increasing roar from a distance. I'd never heard anything like it before. The roar became louder and louder, then reached a crescendo. I asked the guide what the sound was, and he told me it came from many, many monkeys joining in a chorus. Every night, at about the same time, the roar returned and lasted for about 30 minutes.

While we were in the jungle, I did not see an anaconda, the largest snake in the world, but I saw signs of its presence. The guide showed me a track left by one that he concluded was about 23-feet long.

One day we walked in terrific heat and came upon a cluster of three huts, where the inhabitants were preparing monkey stew for dinner. It was not an appetizing sight because the monkey carcass looked very similar to that of a human baby. The scene made me want to move on quickly.

We were in the jungle not far from the Para River when I heard a train approaching. Seemingly out of nowhere, it appeared: a steam locomotive pulling a flat car. At the guide's urging, we all climbed aboard the flat car and took a brief excursion along the river. We had ridden for about five minutes when we came to an abrupt halt, and the engineer and fireman jumped from the locomotive and took off running down the track. They had spied a paca, a large native rat that can grow to 20 pounds; paca is considered a delicacy in the region. In a few minutes, the men returned with their prize.

After the trip, I learned that there had been a rubber boom in the 1920s along a section of the Para River. A series of rapids had necessitated the construction of a short-haul railroad, which helped get the rubber to market. The train had outlasted the rubber boom and still served local needs.

The Brazilian jungle is immense and daunting. More than once I would take in the surroundings and I ask myself, How foolish are you to even consider this undertaking?

During the trip, I met a fellow named G.A. Ferguson, who worked for the Norris Grain Company. Norris Grain was the largest grain dealer in the world and a company with lots of resources. Having succeeded in the grain business, the Norris family ventured into sports in a big way and held significant ownership in Madison Square Garden at one time, a contract to manage Joe Louis, ownership of the Detroit Red Wings hockey club as well as a controlling interest in the New York Rangers hockey club. The family owned thousands of acres in Florida and huge cattle ranches and other property throughout the world.

Mr. Ferguson and I engaged in conversation, and he asked what I was doing in Brazil. I told him that I was thinking about going into the lumber business. He said that his people had been thinking about doing the same thing and that he had a man working here investigating possibilities, but in three years, they had not made much progress.

Our conversations led us to become partners with Norris Grain, and we set out to build a sawmill in Brazil. Because their guy, an American from Florida, could speak Portuguese and had spent considerable time in the region already, we relied upon him to recommend the best place to build the mill, and he said he knew exactly where to build it.

I brought two fellows down from Gilbert, Buck Miller and Blaine Eller, to oversee the actual construction. Using local labor, they went right to work and, despite much language difficulty, built the mill deck. On a later trip, I was quite impressed with the progress.

There were no roads where the mill was located, and all access was by boat. I decided to take a boat trip upriver just to take in the surroundings. Not far upriver from the new mill, we came upon a series of waterfalls, nothing huge mind you, but enough of an impediment that no logs could be floated through them.

Immediately I sought out the so-called "expert" and asked if he was planning to build locks to get around the waterfalls, but he just gave me a blank look. Some expert! Because we couldn't float logs to the mill, what we had built was completely useless. It was clear that we would have to start all over again. When I told Buck Miller that we would have to build another mill, he said, "I want to get my hands on that SOB," referring to the Norris employee, "I want to kick his ass."

I went to the Norris Grain folks and said, "I want out. Either you get out or I get out." So I bought them out. Even though I parted ways with the Norris Grain Company, I remained friends with Mr. Ferguson, who was a really decent and honorable man.

When we were in the midst of building the second mill, I sent three of our local laborers to Belém in our boat to pick up a load of corrugated-asbestos roofing material. It took about a day to get to Belém by boat and a day and a half to two days for the return trip. Those fellows were gone six days before they returned, and I was beside myself with concern. When they finally showed up, I took our interpreter, Moises Oliverio, with me down to the dock to find out what had gone wrong. We asked them where they'd been.

"Belém."

"What took so long?"

Everybody shrugged.

"Well, get this boat unloaded now."

One big fellow seemed offended by my order. Moises translated for me, "He says he is a cook not a stevedore."

"Tell him," I answered, "that he unloads the boat, or he doesn't have a job."

"He won't unload the boat."

"Tell him to give me the keys to the boat. He's fired."

"He won't give us the keys."

I walked back to the mill with Moises and this big obstinate fellow, who was sputtering all kinds of Portuguese and holding the keys tightly in his huge hands. I told Buck Miller, "I think we may have a problem here. I just fired this fellow, but he won't give us the keys to the boat."

I turned to Moises and said, "Tell, him that he has 30 seconds to give us the keys or he is in big trouble." I noticed Buck Miller sneaking up behind the guy with a three-foot wooden club. Just before the fellow turned over the keys, Buck yelled, "Hit him, Buck, and I'll kill the SOB." Thankfully the standoff ended peacefully, and we had no violence that evening.

The second time we got it right. We built a mill near Abetetuba on the Tocantins River, and it turned out to be quite a facility. Still, Brazilian weather made it difficult to succeed. In the rainy season, the soil would turn to mud, making it impossible to work. Eventually, we built a wood floor throughout the entire mill area—about four acres—just so we could operate.

To get logs, I made the craziest deal I've ever made. We found these three fellows who were loggers and advanced them $900,000 to hire workers, buy boats, chainsaws, ropes and supplies. I've often thought how risky that investment was. The fact is I never really knew the fellows who did the logging. Of course, we would check them out as best we could through local authorities, but their guarantee was flimsy at best. It was nearly a year before they delivered any logs. When they finally arrived, I was amazed. However shaky the deal seemed to be, we never got burnt or cheated, and they were always good for their word.

The loggers cut the timber in the dry season, and in the wet season transported the logs downriver, which was sometimes as much as a 500-mile trip. Rafts of logs would appear out of the blue, and there'd be six or eight motorboats guiding the rafts. Whole families would make the trip along with their goats and whatever else they owned. After a seasonal logging job, many of the workers left the deep jungle and headed to Belém, the big city downriver, in hopes of finding a better life. The average annual income in the deep jungle was just $200 a year, the biggest source of income being Brazil nuts and tropical fish.

We'd saw the logs, store the lumber, and when there was sufficient supply, an oceangoing freighter would take on the finished products. We transported our lumber from South America to a dock and warehouse in Mobile, which served as our main distribution point, although in some instances we shipped directly from the mill to the customer. We sold to customers throughout the world, using international brokers to represent us. We sold primarily to the furniture, flooring and cabinetry industries. We had a Canadian customer who purchased two-million board feet at a time—a full ship load—to produce picture frames. Typically we sold large quantities of specific hardwoods to out-of-country operations and delivered by ship. In the U.S., we delivered mostly by rail and by truck some of the time.

Buck Miller and Blaine Eller were essential to our success in Brazil. Buck was the sawyer, and he oversaw the employees and set the work hours. Blaine assisted Buck and was the millwright, the one responsible for installing and maintaining the equipment. We would have never made it without those two.

Buck Miller was the toughest fellow I ever met in my life. He only weighed about 145 pounds, but he wasn't afraid of anything. When I first broached the idea of him going to Brazil to start a sawmill, he looked at me and giggled, "But, Buck, I've never even been out of West Virginia."

"Well," I answered, "This will be a wonderful opportunity. And you won't be on your own altogether because I'll be down there regularly to spend time with you."

He and Blaine stayed for nine years. I'd go down an average of once a month to check on things. At Christmas time, they'd come home for a couple of weeks, and in the summertime when school was out, Buck's family would visit him in Brazil. Blaine was single.

Those two fellows had a rough time of it. When they arrived, they couldn't speak a word of Portuguese and communicated with the locals significantly by hand gestures. We built them a house but stupidly built it on the ground, which allowed rats to move right in. The second house we built on stilts. I eventually found a cook who knew how to prepare American food, and they felt a little better off. But they faced all kinds of hardship.

Once I got a call from our general manager in Belém. "Mr. Harless," he said, "Mr. Miller has been drunk for two weeks, and we can't get any work done."

Larry and I flew to Brazil the next day. When we reached the mill, we found Buck Miller quite drunk and the operation at a near standstill. At dinner that night, I told Buck that I wanted to investigate the river upstream and that I wanted him to go with us. He agreed to make the trip.

My idea was to get Buck away from the whiskey for a while, so that he might decide to put the bottle away and sober up. Buck showed up drunk the next morning and remained drunk the entire day. Both Larry and I watched him closely but could not figure out how or where he was getting his booze. He eventually sobered up but would never tell us how he was able to stay drunk on that boat. I learned that sometimes it's better if you don't know the whole story.

The Brazilian Federal Police raided a house of ill repute in Abetetuba, the village near the mill, and one of the people they found inside was Buck Miller. When the police attempted to make an arrest, Buck took an officer's pistol and ran away in the direction of the mill. The police were afraid to go to the mill to try to make an arrest because I'm sure they were afraid of what Buck might do to them. I came down again and worked with the mayor to ease a tense situation, which involved paying off a few people. Buck was never arrested, and the officer got his gun back. Since he was essential, I know that if I had lost Buck Miller, or if he had given up, I would've pulled the plug on the whole endeavor.

Moises, our first interpreter, was a very sharp young man, who did an excellent job for us in Brazil. Later he became one of our logging contractors, and today, based out of Houston, Texas, he works in the oil industry with companies throughout the world. He recently became a U.S. citizen. When I celebrated my 90th birthday with a big party in Charleston, Moises was in attendance. It was really good to see him.

Our second interpreter was named Virgil, and he was in another class altogether. I'm convinced that Virgil was a former Nazi, who was hiding out in Brazil. Some war criminals and others with unsavory pasts found their way to South America after World War II. Virgil fit the profile very well. He was from Germany, lived up the river away from the big cities, married a Brazilian girl and fathered several children. Of course, none of that raised our suspicions. What did, however, was his practice of goose-step walking. Virgil walked exactly the way German soldiers marched during Hitler's reign. His manner of walking gave one the distinct impression that he somehow held onto a defeated past. Still, the difficulty of finding someone who could speak English, as well as the local dialect, left us no choice but to accept his odd behavior. Besides, we had no proof of a nefarious past.

When I was in Gilbert, I kept in touch with Virgil by telephone. Since we rarely had a good connection, my conversations with him weren't always understandable. I was at a meeting at The Greenbrier one day, and Ruth Phipps, who was my secretary at the time, called and said, "I can't tell for sure, Mr. Harless, but I think Virgil is saying that the dock fell in."

Oh God, I thought, we've got two-million board feet of lumber sitting on that dock. It would be devastating if we lost that inventory. Later in the day, we finally made a follow-up connection with Virgil. "How's it going?" I asked.

"Oh, fine."

"Good! We must have misunderstood that the dock had collapsed."

"Oh, it collapsed alright, but everything is fine." Virgil was a good interpreter able to use perfect English. However, you can tell by his response that he wasn't very smart, or at the very least, was entirely unconcerned.

Two-million board feet of lumber made its way down the river, and we were unable to salvage any of it! About four months of work just floated away.

We had our share of heartaches in Brazil.

It was not uncommon for us to purchase lumber from other mills in order to fill a ship. On one occasion, we flew to a mill, and I made the mistake of not taking any water with me. Drinking the local water was not advised, so I inquired if there was a local restaurant where I could get a cold drink. Our guide directed me to a little restaurant with a small counter and three or four booths. I sat down at the counter and ordered a soft drink. In one of the booths, sat a fellow who looked like he might be an American, so I struck up a conversation with him. It turned out that he was an American, and I asked him what part of the country he hailed from.

"West Virginia," he responded.

"Really," I exclaimed, happy to meet another mountaineer, "where in West Virginia?"

"Oh, a little place in the southern part of the state. You probably wouldn't know it."

"Try me."

"West Hamlin," he said.

"Goodness, I've been through West Hamlin many times on trips to and from Huntington. I'm Buck Harless from Gilbert."

"John Walden," he replied. "Doctor John Walden."

Does anyone need further proof that it is a small world? In a little village in Brazil, I chanced to meet John Walden, M.D., who had spent months in Ecuador and Brazil seeking answers to why the local Indians tended to die at an early age. He told me that he had recently finished a round of research and was waiting for a boat to take him downriver to Belém to catch a flight on his return to the U.S.

He accepted my offer to fly him to Belém, and on the flight there, he told me that he had run out of cash and had only credit cards, which had been of no use in the jungle. He looked forward to Belém where credit cards were "good as gold."

Our paths have continued to cross over the years and Dr. Walden has done wonderful work in his field of study. Today he is chairman of the Department of Family and Community Health at the Joan C. Edwards School of Medicine at Marshall University in Huntington.

We had operated in Brazil for about three years when we had to fire the general manager because of dishonesty. This was a very bad situation since it was extremely difficult to find someone in a foreign country capable of doing the job we needed done. Not only did the right person have to be experienced in the lumber business, but he had to be honest, understand the people and customs and speak the language. After much searching, I found a talented man who was working at a mill in Bolivia. He was an Englishman named George Robinson, and I traveled to La Paz to speak with him face to face.

La Paz, Bolivia, is the highest capital city in the world situated over 12,000 feet above sea level. I arrived at the airport at 8:30 p.m. and made my way down to the city and my hotel. I say down because the airport is 13,000 feet above sea level. I checked into my hotel without a problem and had a bite to eat. Being tired, I headed straight to my room and to bed, but I had trouble sleeping. I found myself waking up and gasping for air. Thinking that my condition was associated to the high altitude, I called the front desk and asked what could be done for guests who were experiencing this problem.

"Weren't you given an oxygen tank when you checked in?" the clerk asked.

"No."

"I'll send you one immediately."

Moments later, a hotel staffer appeared with an oxygen tank and mask and showed me how to use it. With the additional oxygen, I got a reasonable night's sleep.

I was to meet Mr. Robinson the following day, but he did not appear. That evening I went to dinner by myself at a restaurant about five blocks from the hotel. As I was leaving the restaurant, there was a huge explosion a block away. I knew that something bad had happened and thought it best for me to return to my hotel. Once inside the lobby, I was approached by a man who identified himself as a reporter from a newspaper in Columbia.

"Aren't you an American?" he asked.

"Yes."

"I will give some advice. If I were you, I would not be on the streets at night. They just blew up the American Embassy. There are people here who are very angry at the American government and the American people."

"Goodness," I responded, "I heard the explosion, but I

didn't know what it was." I kept a low profile for the rest of my stay.

George Robinson showed up the next day, and we came to terms quickly. About three weeks later, George and his wife, Lilly, arrived at the mill and moved into the house we had there. He turned out to be an excellent hire and later worked for us in Guatemala.

During the time we were in Brazil, I was youth director at the Gilbert Presbyterian Church. I introduced a contest to the children, offering a trip to Brazil for the ones who learned the most about the Bible. I gave them Bible verses to memorize, starting out with familiar ones like the Lord's Prayer and progressing to more difficult verses. The contest ended with the 51st chapter of Isaiah. Two youngsters, Tim Rutledge and Debbie Cline, excelled in the exercises and were chosen by their peers to make the trip to Brazil. June and I chaperoned the youngsters, who were excited to be visiting a foreign country.

Our church in Gilbert had provided financial support over time to an orphanage in Brazil, and one of the highlights of the children's trip was to visit the orphanage, which was about 150 miles from our mill. On the morning we were to leave to visit the orphanage, I got a call from the mill telling me that it was on fire. A small fire had started on the dock, and workers hurried to the fire hose hoping to quickly extinguish the flames. They didn't know that the hose had been recently used to pump diesel fuel and that it still contained a sizeable amount of diesel. The first attempt to quench the flames served to swell the fire spectacularly. Water eventually flushed out the remaining diesel, and they were able to extinguish the blaze. The fire caused quite a mess, and because of it, the children did not get to make the trip to the orphanage.

In 1974, the Session of the Gilbert Presbyterian Church decided to remodel the church interior, which had become unattractive and uncomfortable. The pews were easily more than 80-years old and much of the plaster in the sanctuary was in disrepair. Everybody agreed it needed freshening up. We were milling in Brazil, and I donated mahogany lumber for the remodeling. The pews and other items in the sanctuary were crafted using Brazilian mahogany. Charles Peake, Jr. was chairman of the committee overseeing the project. Charles did an admirable job and worked diligently to ensure a high-quality outcome. Late in the process, though, he was diagnosed with a serious form of cancer and died before the project was completed. He would have been proud of the finished sanctuary. All of us were.

Altogether we had three mills that we operated in South and Central America at different times: Ecuador, Brazil and Guatemala.

The Guatemalan mill was very modern and had top-quality logging equipment with Caterpillar D6 dozers, nice forklifts and a six-foot band mill. We sawed beautiful mahogany exclusively. The mill's general manager, George Robinson, was an expatriate Brit who could've passed as an American. He had made friends with the governor of the province, who was facing re-election, and George recommended that we contribute to the governor's campaign. We contributed, but he lost the election. A couple of weeks later, armed goons appeared at the mill and shut it down. George escaped to Guatemala City, where he called Larry, who told him to lay low and not try to go back. It wasn't long before the government confiscated our mill and we were completely out of business in Guatemala.

During the Vietnam War, many ocean freighters were dedicated to the war effort. At one point, we couldn't find ships to haul our lumber, so we purchased two 5,000-ton tramp steamers. We hauled lumber from Brazil to Mobile, and on the return trip, we'd carry scrap iron for $11 a ton from Houston, Texas, to Venezuela and other ports. About a month after the war ended, the price of scrap iron tanked to $4 a ton, a price well below our operating cost, and we had to sell our ships. One ship we sold rather quickly; the other took forever. Finally, movie producers seeking a ship for a film, rented it, painted it black and featured it in the movie The Ghost Ship.

We were in Brazil for 10 years, and I'm proud to say that we were the only American company to make a go of it down there and make a profit. No other company did, even very large companies, including Georgia Pacific, Weyerhaeuser and Potlatch. All of them had trouble keeping managers who were willing to work in that environment. We had Buck Miller and Blaine Eller, and of course, I was there frequently. Altogether, our enterprise in South America was quite an experience, but it is not something I would want to try again—even if I was a good deal younger.

I was back in Brazil not long ago because I wanted to reminisce and to show the mill to my wife, Hallie, and to give her a greater understanding of how it worked. Terry Sammons and his wife, Penny, accompanied us. We flew to Belém and drove on a newly-constructed highway to Abetetuba. When we operated in Abetetuba, the only access was by water or air. The changes were quite substantial. Abetetuba has grown from 2,200 people, when I was first there, to about 30,000, and I hardly recognized a thing. I asked people if they knew where the old Mafina mill was (Mafina was our company name), and no one was familiar with the name. We took a taxi, but I could not find the old mill site. The next day, I hired an airplane, and from the air, we were able to identify its location.

After the flight, we hailed another taxi to drive us to the mill. The taxi and its driver were not very clean, and Terry and Penny seemed quite uncomfortable in a dirty taxi driven by such an unsavory-looking character. At one point, we stopped and asked an old man if he knew where the old Mafina mill was, and he directed us to the site. A French company now owns our old facility and operates a considerably downsized operation, a small dimension mill. However, it still uses our old house for an office.

That trip brought back many memories.

In addition to shipping lumber on the world market, we had wholesale lumber stores throughout the southern and western U.S. The first was in El Paso, Texas, and we opened stores in North Carolina, Arizona and Georgia, a total of seven stores altogether.

A customer in Memphis, Tennessee, told Larry about a casket company in El Paso that was for sale and suggested that it might be a good deal for us. Larry and I visited the plant to consider the purchase, but it seems that I did not make a good first impression on the employees. At the time, I was wearing a neck brace due to a pinched nerve in my neck and had been suffering excruciating pain for some time. Apparently the neck brace and my pained demeanor made me appear as some sort of pathetic character, and the workers thought that I was there to pick out a casket in anticipation of my worldly demise.

We purchased the casket company, although we clearly did not do enough research before doing so. We later learned that casket-making was a cottage industry throughout the region and that there was an abundant supply of simple wood caskets at better prices than we could produce. We got out of the casket business after about a year, even though we continued to supply lumber to the new owners.

Months later, a Catholic funeral was held and the deceased was laid out in a wood casket made by the company that we had recently sold. During the procession, as the casket was being carried down a long flight of steps to the hearse, the bottom of the casket broke apart and the body fell out and rolled down the remaining steps to the sidewalk. The deceased's relatives were horrified, and to make matters worse, the corpse wore no pants. The aggrieved family sued the undertaker, the casket company and us since we had supplied the lumber to make the casket. Fortunately, the court dismissed us from the suit.

When we returned to the lumber business in the Appalachian territory, we entered into a joint agreement with Pocahontas Land Corporation*, a subsidiary of Norfolk Southern Corporation, and built new mills in Gilbert, in the Charleston area and in Duffield, Virginia. The new mills in Gilbert and Duffield were built specifically to produce railroad ties for Norfolk Southern. Our mill in Duffield was our biggest and most technologically advanced with an output of 12,000 feet per hour. That's one and a half times more than I did in 10 hours when I first started sawmilling. In fact, 8,000 feet was a big day for me early on—a very big day. Our other mills were very sophisticated as well.

About all of our lumber business over the years was in hardwoods: oak, cherry, maple, hickory and the like. Early on I sawed some hemlock, which is plentiful in the Appalachian territory and can be used for house framing. In fact, all of the framing in the house that I lived in most of my life is hemlock. It's the best wood framing you can get because termites will not eat it.

It used to be that 80 percent of our production went to North Carolina, Virginia and Tennessee. Over time, it changed to 70 percent for export to countries like China, England, Spain, Portugal and Vietnam. The lumber industry continues to change. Red oak, for example, which had been a staple for years and years, is not fashionable today, and its price has plummeted. Maple has replaced it as the best seller.

Compared to a few years ago, only 25% of U.S. furniture manufacturers survive. The U.S. has lost 75% of its furniture manufacturing to Indonesia and China. North Carolina once had a large number of furniture manufacturers, but the survivors are moving or have moved lock, stock and barrel to China. Several companies that did not move their operations are mostly out of business.

We had a sales manager who traveled throughout the world, selling lumber and visiting our representatives in different locales. He returned from a trip to China, telling me about one furniture plant he visited near Shanghai that employed thousands of people. It operated three shifts a day and had the most modern equipment, just as modern as anything in this country.

Later I got to see the factory for myself when I went to China with a group of West Virginia University supporters called the Blue and Gold Travelers. While we were in Shanghai, Scott England, our sales manager, made arrangements for me to visit the factory. We left the city and traveled about two hours before coming upon a huge complex of brick buildings. During the tour that the company provided, I saw a factory as modern and sophisticated as any in the United States. The company representative took me to a warehouse where Gilco Lumber—our brand—was waiting to be turned into furniture.

The factory, one of the largest of its type in China, was built and managed by individuals from Taiwan. The plant representative explained that cheap labor costs were the primary reason that the factory was in China and not Taiwan. They housed some 7,000 workers on the plant premises and were seeking an additional 3,000 workers. Pay was $150 a month with $15 a month deducted for room and board. Each worker typically worked a 10-hour day, but since they were on a quota system, if the required work was not completed in 10 hours, they worked as long as necessary to fulfill the production goal. Of course the U.S. worker cannot compete with his Chinese counterpart on these terms, and the technology that was once our competitive edge is equalizing.

I asked our host what would happen if the rate of pay in China would increase to the high rates paid in Taiwan, itself once a low-paying location, and was told that the owners would move the plant to an area where rates of pay were low. It is no wonder that the U.S. no longer has a viable furniture industry.

We could ship products from Norfolk, Virginia to China cheaper than we could ship lumber from here to California or even Chicago. There were so many products coming from Asia in container ships to the U.S. that there was a huge surplus of containers waiting for the return trip to Asia, making freight costs of shipping to Asia relatively low. Increases in shipping rates, driven by the rising cost of petroleum, gave those of us wanting a healthy furniture industry in the U.S. some level of hope that conditions might become more favorable. But a sober, realistic assessment lead to the conclusion that the deteriorating market for hardwoods would force us to cut back on production significantly or even cause us to leave the marketplace altogether.

Faced with these conditions and advanced age, I sought a positive way to extricate myself from the lumber business, something that had been a big part of me since 1947. I wanted to find a buyer who would keep as many employees as possible, since good employees have been critical to our success. A local entrepreneur and gentleman, Everett Hannah, has been able to purchase all of our lumber assets and keep most of the employees working.

After the sale, I don't know if people expected me to go into a deep depression or what, but I admit it is a little strange to no longer be in the lumber business. I believe I sold to the right man for the right reasons and that he will strive to keep local people employed. I wish him well, and I thank God for the opportunities given me and hope that in His view that I lived up to His trust in me. I know that I tried.

* At the time, Bob Raines was president of Pocahontas Land Corporation, and he became a good friend over the years. In fact, lease agreements we worked out with Bob not only increased our lumber business but aided our activities in the coal business too, first with Jumacris Mining and later with Hampden Coal Company.

Bob also assisted in creating the Hatfield and McCoy Trail, a popular trail-riding venture that uses access roads, many belonging to Pocahontas Land, in very rugged sections of southern West Virginia for four-wheeling excursions. Four wheeling on the Hatfield and McCoy Trail has gained national recognition and has been a boon for local mom-and-pop-style businesses.

I got the promoters together with Bob in the early planning stages and helped overcome concerns about liability by bringing in John Fisher of the West Virginia University Law School, who drafted legislation regarding liability limitations. The bill became law and the Hatfield and McCoy Trail has exceeded almost everyone's expectations.

Bob and I chuckle about that first meeting with the promoters, Mike Whitt and Leff Moore, because their plan was audacious and seemingly unobtainable. We both recall, after the introductions, he laughed and said, "Buck, if you weren't with these fellows, I would throw them out of my office."

Many people made the Hatfield and McCoy Trail a reality. I'm happy to have played a role. People working together can do things that may seem impossible at first.

Chapter Ten

Friends and I formed DASH Coal Company as a means of spending more time together. DASH was made up using the first letters of the four incorporators' last names: John Davis, Frank Alara, Fred Shewey, and James Harless. We each put up $3,000 to capitalize a business that started out on somewhat of a whim. John Davis didn't stay with us very long because his frequent trips to Gilbert made his wife believe that he was up to hanky panky of some sort, and the issue was straining the marriage. He came to me one day and said that he had to get out, so each of the remaining partners paid John $1,000 to buy his share.

In the beginning, we had limited success, but DASH Coal grew larger than any of us anticipated and became a very successful endeavor. We were once offered $65 million for what became of that $12,000 original investment, but it took a while—and a little luck—to get to that value.

At first we leased a seam of coal from the Mingo-Wyoming Coal Land Company, whose president was Rolla D. Campbell, a very distinguished attorney from Huntington. He came to Gilbert to iron out the details of the lease with me, and a few days later, I received a printed copy. In it was the unique stipulation that I could be paid no more than $500 a month throughout the term of the lease as manager of the operation.

I knew that there was no legal basis for that provision, but I signed the lease as written, and we started producing coal using contractors to do the mining.

Each contractor produced about 100 tons a day, all by hand loading and by "shooting off the solid," blasting coal that had not been undercut. It's a blasting technique that was lawful at the time but illegal today. We paid the contractors $3.00 a ton and sold the coal for $4.00 a ton. The lease called for payment of 25 cents per ton to the property owners. Finally, we paid 25 cents per ton to get it loaded onto railcars, so our gross profit was 50 cents a ton.

I secured additional leases from Western Pocahontas Corporation, which was the holding company for the C&O Railroad at that time. Fred Toothman was a vice president for C&O, and he negotiated the leases. C&O leased us property for 25 cents a ton of coal that we mined, and we were obligated to pay the property taxes.

In the early days, we kind of scraped by, but the price of coal started moving upward and we started making bigger and bigger money. When prices skyrocketed, Toothman told me, "Buck, you're the luckiest fellow I ever saw. You could fall into a shithouse and come out wearing a clean suit of clothes."

The fact is, at the time we secured the leases, Western Pocahontas couldn't give away the property that we leased from them. We signed at the right time, so luck played a role. When the Arab oil embargo hit during the early '70s, coal sold for as much as a $100 a ton. We never got more than $50 a ton for our coal, and our cost was about $13. I thought that was enough profit.

We leased land from corporate land owners and paid them a fee per ton of coal mined. Most of the coal we mined were seams 30- to 40-inches high with 40 to 50% rejects, meaning up to half of what was mined is just rock. One time we had a small lease for an eight-foot seam with only 20% rejects, a coal seam comparable to the early days of mining in southern West Virginia.

Our mining business grew over the years, not in a straight-line fashion, more like two steps forward and one step back. Sometimes it was two steps back and hold on tight.

Garland Brewer was the superintendent of Jumacris Mining, and he was the most unusual person. He was one of the best coal miners I've ever met, yet he threw the most violent fits on the job. I would often talk to him about his behavior. "Garland, you'll have all the men hating you!"

He'd answer, "Buck, they don't pay any attention to my outbursts. They like me." In the final analysis, he was right. The men did like him, and his employees produced more coal per man-hour than miners do today.

I've learned that whatever success I've had in business goes back to good, dedicated employees and managers. Bruce Burgess, my former son-in-law, was superintendent of our strip operation. Eddie Grimmet was with me since graduating from high school. Terry Sammons was our chief engineer. Garland Brewer, of course, was superintendent of Jumacris Mining. They met with me every afternoon at about 4:30 when I was in town. We'd discuss the day's activities, the progress and the problems. Those meetings were good for us because they caused us to be united in a way that made us more like a strong family than an ordinary company. When we grew larger, there simply wasn't the time to spend with the supervisors the way I would like. I miss those meetings.

When I was a young man, all mines were unionized. Back then the general public had a much more positive view of coal mining. It wasn't until the '70s, when the environmental movement became very active and vocal, that coal took on such a negative connotation.

In 1969 and again in 1976, coal mining laws became much stricter and the industry became highly regulated. When I first started in mining, at a surface mine, we just pushed the overburden over the mountain. We can't do anything like that now. Regulations are very strict, and that's the way it should be. Of course in the early days, we were getting only small amounts for a ton of coal. Under the current regulations, we can't mine coal at prices that we used to receive. It's a simple matter of economics. As restrictions and environmental concerns grew stronger, the price of coal went up. It had to.

With any form of mining, it is impossible to collect pure coal. Rock, commonly referred to as slate, is a by-product of mining and is mixed with the coal when it is mined. Since coal is lighter than rock, it can be made to float in water, and coal washers at preparation plants separate the rock from the coal before it is shipped to the customer.

Years ago, it was commonplace to take slate, the rock left over from mining, and use it as fill material to build up and level property. Around Gilbert there is precious little flat land, and someone would be foolhardy to build a home on sloping land along a river that is prone to flooding. So common practice was to use slate to fill and level property for building. Meade's Shopping Center in Gilbert and my sawmill were built on filled-in land. In fact, the property where I now live was filled in and built up that way.

I owned a piece of flood-prone land near my sawmill in Gilbert and decided to do something about it. In 1980, I set out to build it up above the floodplain. I used a bulldozer to push rock and gravel out of the Guyandotte River and fashioned a retaining wall where my property adjoined the river. Next, I used slate from our coal preparation plant to fill in the void behind the retaining wall. I was respectful of the river, and at no time did I place or allow slate to get into its waters. I knew it was a misdemeanor offense to have a bulldozer in the river, which usually carried a fine of about $100, but since I was improving the land, I believed it was reasonable to risk the small fine. I turned out to be gravely mistaken.

One day I got a letter from a colonel in the U.S. Army Corps of Engineers in Huntington, telling me to cease and desist from dumping slate into the river. The Colonel's letter also referred to the Guyandotte as a "navigable stream." I wrote back a very smart-assed letter, stating that I hadn't dumped any slate into the river and that I hadn't seen any steamboats on the river lately either. Smart assed and dumb I was.

Days later a U.S. Marshal walked into my office in Gilbert with nine warrants with my name on them. Nine warrants for felonies! (I was told at the time that I was the only individual who had been personally indicted under the

Rivers and Harbors Act of 1895. Corporations had been indicted, but not an individual.)

I retained the law firm of Jackson Kelly to represent me, and much to my surprise, they recommended that I plead guilty to three of the counts. I said, "But, I haven't done what they claim." I took my attorneys over to the site that I had built with the bulldozer. "Here, look," I complained, "there's no way that slate can get into the river." But they finally convinced me to plead guilty.

First I went before Maurice Taylor, a federal magistrate and a good friend of mine, who set a court date. One of Maurice's relatives mistakenly thought that the magistrate had put me in jail. Livid, she called him and gave him a terrible tongue-lashing before he could explain that it had only been a procedural hearing and that I was not in jail.

Next was an appearance in U.S. District Court in Charleston before Judge Charles Haden. "Mr. Harless," the judge intoned, "you are accused of so and so of the U.S Code. Three counts. Are you guilty?"

"Yes, your honor."

"Mr. Harless," he inquired, "do you know that I can fine you $25,000 on each of these three counts and send you to jail for five years for each one of them? Now, do you still want to plead guilty?" He was making sure that I understood what I was doing, and frankly, I was simply following my attorney's instructions.

"Yes sir, I know," I answered.

"OK," he told the government lawyer, "I'm going to accept this man's guilty plea, but he can withdraw his plea if the Army Corps doesn't give him a permit within 90 days. If it doesn't, then he can come back to this court and withdraw his guilty pleas." With the order, the judge set conditions for the parties to end the dispute: I was to apply properly for a permit to do the work that I had already carried out and the Army Corps was to grant the permit.

For whatever reason, the Corps of Engineers did not grant me a permit within the 90-day time frame, and on the 91st day after Judge Haden's ruling, my attorneys appeared before him and withdrew my guilty pleas.

The lawyer who represented the Army Corps, a Ms. Fienberg, apparently had been preparing for trial. She called one of my lawyers at Jackson Kelly, expressing dismay with her client. My lawyer told me about their conversation: "She was so mad my phone was smoking. She said, 'Those sons-of-bitches lied to me. I've learned from their own records that your client didn't do what they accused him of doing. So, I'm withdrawing the complaint, and I'm going to try to get somebody fired!'"

There had been negative headlines in the papers; I had spent thousands of dollars in legal fees and additional thousands in engineering fees, and the government dropped its case. At the time, I was Moderator of the Greenbrier Presbytery of the Presbyterian Church USA. In the Sunday edition of *The Charleston Gazette and Mail*, a headline read "Moderator of Church Indicted." Of course, that's all most people remember. They don't know that the case was dropped, and the *Gazette* did not run a big headline proclaiming "Indictment Dropped."

In terms of safety, environmental stewardship and land management, the coal industry does a better job than ever before, but it's not held in high regard by many people. For example, there are those who are adamantly opposed to surface mining, even though I believe such mining can be carried out in a responsible manner. We've got a surface mine nearby that looks like a moon landscape right now. When we get done with that job, it will be green and attractive, but it looks awful now because it can't be helped. When that much soil is disturbed, it's going look bad until it is reclaimed. Yet, environmentalists emphasize these pre-reclamation jobs, and rarely show a completed job where the reclamation is well executed.

The coal industry has accepted the rules and regulations because most are responsible operators, who want to do minimum harm to the environment. You know, most of us are environmentalists in the sense that we don't want to see things destroyed, see timber burn or see the landscape devastated. Regulation has been very expensive, but the industry has adapted. Where we have failed—and it's not because we haven't tried—is in getting our message across to the public. We've improved understanding somewhat, but a negative image still exists. Environmentalists were right in their criticisms of early surface mining techniques. Those methods were wrong, and they should have been stopped.

The harshest criticisms are against mountain top removal mining. I think it's a shame how some people exaggerate its impact. They claim it causes flooding, but that's not true at all. In fact, the way they build ponds around those mountaintops helps to prevent flooding. Southern West Virginia needs flat land, and prudent and strategic mountain top removal mining can help fill that need. In addition the state needs the mining industry. Our state government has had budget surpluses recently, and they are attributable largely to the coal industry.

Today, big players dominate the West Virginia coal industry, and we have significantly fewer independent owners. The Jones family, Jim Justice, Tracy Hylton, Lawson Hamilton,

Jim Compton and I were successful independent coal operators, and all of us have donated a bunch of money since the early '70s, primarily for education. The big corporations don't seem to be quite as generous as the independents; we live in the state and want to improve the quality of life here.

Good coal miners are necessary for a coal operator's success, but the skills required of a coal miner today are much more technical in nature than before. Years ago a boy who graduated from high school generally had the goal of being a miner like his dad. A lot of times, he'd go to work with his dad who would teach him, and the young man would become a skilled miner. Of course we didn't have the equipment then that we've got now. Today it's high-tech stuff and our biggest problem is finding skilled people who can work on this complex equipment.

I was at a surface mine where my brother, Jimmy, is superintendent. He had a loader out of commission, a big loader. The cost of the machine was over $1.75 million. A skilled mechanic had been working on the loader all day, trying to find out why it wouldn't run. He was using a sophisticated computer that was supposed to be able to diagnose the problem, but the computer was unable to do so. So this fellow relied upon his skills and experience to troubleshoot the problem himself. People who understand these very expensive machines better than computers are in extremely short supply.

We had $25 million worth of equipment at a surface mine operation, and half of it was sitting idle because we couldn't get the necessary explosives to shoot the overburden. We were able to get only 75% of what we needed. If it wasn't one thing, it was another. We spent over $5 million getting a site ready in nearby Horsepen, and after all of that preparation, we weren't sure that we could mine coal there because of unstable roof conditions. There are so many factors that go into coal mining. I think that it is safe to say that more companies have gone broke in the coal business than have made it.

Coal mining is a very difficult business that operates in generally unstable market conditions. In March of 2003, I concluded that we were going to have to get out of the coal business. We had been losing $300,000 to $400,000 every month and things were looking pretty grim. Hoping that conditions might change, we decided to wait until June, and we kept putting off the final decision month after month until the end of the year. The real heartache was the concern of losing a lot of good people, good employees with families to support. By the end of December, thank goodness, conditions got better, and we didn't have to shut down.

I believe that the future of coal is in its conversion to gasoline and diesel. This is happening elsewhere already. In South Africa 25% of its energy is from liquid fuel made from coal. I understand that conversion is economically feasible when oil is $40 a barrel or above, and it is way above that benchmark now. While it's easier to make diesel from coal, gasoline can be made from it as well, and both are becoming more and more expensive. If the U.S. doesn't make a strategic commitment to invest and further perfect coal-conversion technology, I believe we're just wasting time before catastrophe strikes. Far too much crude comes from unstable regions and countries that hate us. We're at their mercy, and our backs are against the wall.

Chapter Eleven

After June died, I was a pretty lonely fellow. She had suffered so much in her final years that her death was ultimately a blessing, but something important was torn from me when she breathed her last breath. Grief is a necessary but very lonely experience. Gone was the familiarity of so many years together, and the result was a huge emptiness. I found it almost impossible to bounce back with a cheerful spirit. Going home at night to an empty house was more than difficult; it was sad. I found solace in work and was grateful to have friends who really cared, but I still grieved. To get back to living, I had to work through the loss, a moment, an hour and a day at a time. After a while I began to heal.

I did not begin to cook for myself, however. Instead, I took my meals at different restaurants in and around Gilbert. Sometimes I would drive to Logan to eat, and sometimes for my evening meal, I would go to the Justonian Restaurant in Justice, where I started having enjoyable conversations with its owner, Hallie Chapman. I had actually known Hallie in passing for years, having first met her when she was a 15-year-old waitress at the Kiwanis Club in Gilbert.

Hallie and I would talk about our youth, friends and school days: all the things that people tend to reminisce about. I learned that she was the youngest of 10 kids, five boys and five girls. As the youngest, she rarely got new clothes, and she wore mostly hand-me-downs. She told me that they all bathed in a metal washtub, something I did when I was a kid. Being the youngest, she was always the last one in the tub, and her sisters would kid her by whispering that they had peed in the water. Hallie would cry, but her mom would make her bathe in the same water anyway. She said the kids were always arguing, and with 10 in a brood, how could they not? One Saturday, her dad lost his patience and told them that tomorrow things were going to be different. When the family got home from church, he announced, "I've figured out a way to settle these arguments, so from here on, I'm going to let you fight it out." Whenever any of them got into a big argument, he'd say, "OK, Sunday after church, we're going to put the gloves on." True to his word, he would bring out the boxing gloves and let them battle it out. In fact, he would make them. I suspect that the arguments diminished considerably in time.

For three months, I guess, I had my meals at Hallie's restaurant, and we would sit and talk, sometimes for an hour or more, even though it always seemed like minutes. Eventually I asked her if she would like to go to dinner and a movie, and she agreed. We had a good time that night and started dating, but I had no idea that it was going to develop into anything serious. Goodness, I was 81 years old! But we discovered that we were very compatible; the main thing is that we can talk about anything under the sun.

One evening we took a leisurely drive down to the sawmill, so I could check on things there. Along the way, Hallie asked, "What are you looking for in a partner? Love and companionship, or sex?"

I said, "Both, depending upon how you separate the two." I think that surprised her, but I also think she was pleased.

When people discovered that we were planning to get married, most thought that she was making a move for my money. Before we tied the knot—at her insistence—we signed a prenuptial agreement; she did not want anything. I said to her, "You know, I'm getting older, and you may have problems down the road looking after me and caring for me. Let me change my will and put some money in it for you."

Her response was, "Absolutely not!"

When we got married, I gave her a credit card, but it was two years before she used it for the first time. She is not extravagant, but she plays the lottery consistently, buying 10 tickets every weekend, rain or shine.

Hallie has both undergraduate and graduate degrees in education from Marshall University. Amazingly, she commuted from Justice to Huntington throughout her entire college career, a round trip of about 230 miles, because her mother was sick during those years. She didn't want to be away from her and wanted to be able to help her mom at night. Her devotion speaks admirably to her character. Hallie taught science in Mingo County schools for 18 years, and during that time, she bought the Justonian Restaurant, which is considered one of the best eating establishments in the area.

I'll tell you this: Hallie is an independent woman who is able to hold her own in any situation, and I respect her for it. If I start making suggestions regarding her restaurant, she'll say, "I've been in this business for 22 years. You take care of coal mines and sawmills, and I'll take care of the restaurant." We don't argue about it. I know how far I can go, and we laugh about the rest of it.

She loves to fish and I do too. She gets so excited when she catches one that she'll squeal and carry on. I'll never forget the first time I took her sail fishing off Costa Rica. She hooked a large sailfish, and it took about 30 minutes for her to reel it in. She was so excited that I thought she was going to throw the rod and reel into the ocean.

I yelled, "Hallie, Hallie, wind it, wind it."

She was screaming, "I got one! I got one!" And damn, she sure did.

We play golf together on occasion. I once took her to a course in Logan, and on the first tee, she smacked the ball almost 230 yards, ending up about 35 yards short of the green. I made a quick mental note to not place any bets with her. However, I found out that, like most golfers, she tries to kill the ball every time. On the succeeding holes, she sprayed shots here and there, but, boy, that first shot was perfect. In sports, she plays to win and hates to lose.

Hallie likes to travel with me. We've been to mainland China, Japan and Hong Kong. Also to France, Greece, Italy, Portugal, Gibraltar and all over South America. We've taken a cruise to Alaska, which was absolutely stunning, and visited Yellowstone Park and Mount Rushmore.

We live a very simple life. We regularly attend church and every once in a while dine out at a little place called Tops in Stollings. Tops serves the best steaks I've had anywhere. Their steaks are three-quarters of an inch thick and cooked just right, exactly to order every time, and, no, I have no financial interest in Tops whatsoever.

Today, Hallie is outside mowing the lawn because she wants to do it. She's a worker and I've never heard her complain. About the only luxury that she allows herself—if you can call it that—is that she hires someone to do the laundry and housecleaning.

She babies me and watches out for my well being. I could not have found a more compatible person than Hallie, and if you get the idea that I'm quite smitten by her, I must confess that you are completely right.

Hallie has three children from two earlier marriages. Her older son, Ryan, is a captain in the U.S. Marine Corps; her other son, Brett, is a graduate of West Virginia University with a degree in business administration; and her daughter, Racina, studied at WVU-Tech, in Montgomery before pursuing studies in cosmetology.

Not long ago, Racina fell and hurt her hip, and the next day, she walked with a limp and was sore and bruised at the point of impact. Hallie advised her to see a doctor to have the hip examined to ascertain the extent of the injury. On Monday, at a hospital in Beckley where she went for x-rays, she exhibited a significantly elevated temperature and was admitted and administered intravenous antibiotics, yet her condition worsened. What began as a simple-looking minor accident soon became a nightmare, and we were helpless bystanders, struggling to make sense of what was happening.

She was airlifted to Ruby Memorial Hospital, the medical center at the West Virginia University School of Medicine, and by Wednesday evening, she was showing some signs of improvement. But in the early hours of Thursday, she weakened and slowly, sadly left this world.

I don't have the words to adequately describe the devastation that Hallie and her boys felt. None of this made enough sense to have any basis for understanding. I grieved for Racina and felt so sad for Hallie, the woman who had given life and breath to this child who had become such a beautiful, vibrant young woman.

Once again, we are reminded of the fragility of life. Coming to terms with such loss will be more than difficult.

Chapter Twelve

My first foray into politics was in 1944 when I ran for mayor of Gilbert against Wirt Hatfield, the gentleman who owned the first radio in Gilbert. I got time off from my job at Red Jacket for a couple of days to go door-to-door to solicit votes. On Election Day, I was up at dawn and spent the entire day greeting everyone who came out to vote. After the polls closed, I was sitting outside the polling place talking with friends, when it suddenly dawned on me that I had not voted. Wouldn't you know it: I lost by one vote!

My first involvement in statewide politics was in 1956 when Cecil Underwood, who was running for governor in the Republican primary, visited my office. He was a member of the West Virginia House of Delegates and was running an underdog campaign against Charleston Mayor John Copenhaver. I was impressed with Cecil: he was young and energetic, and he articulated the issues in ways that were sensible to me. I contributed $500 to his campaign, which was a whole lot of money for me then. He later confided, "You know, if you hadn't given me that $500, we would not have been able to pay for a hotel room in Williamson that night."

I attended an Underwood rally in Kermit, and it was there that I first met Fred Shewey, who would become my dear friend and business partner. The Underwood campaign of 1956 was filled with excitement. Underwood bested Copenhaver in the primary and pulled a stunning upset over U.S. Representative Robert Mollohan in the general election. Cecil Underwood became the youngest governor in West Virginia's history and the first Republican governor in 30 years. I got a taste of statewide politics and, at the same time, made two really good friends.

Cecil, whom I considered a very honorable man, had limited success as governor mainly because the state was struggling financially, and government was a sort of hand-to-mouth operation. But he did some good things with limited tax receipts. He improved the state highways and was very strong on education, but the main thing was that he led a clean administration.

Cecil was again elected governor at age 74 in 1996 and thereby gained the distinction of being West Virginia's youngest and oldest governor. In his second term, he expanded computer technology in public schools and throughout state government. Above all, his was a very honest administration.

Cecil died at age 86, and at his passing, even his political adversaries spoke highly of him, emphasizing his leadership skills and acknowledging his fine character. He was a truly genuine man who sought only betterment for his fellow citizens.

In 1958, Fred Shewey was elected to the Mingo County Board of Education, which made him the first Republican to be elected to any Mingo County office since 1928. At that time, all jobs in Mingo County schools were essentially for sale. "Blind

Bill" Adair was a school board member and county Democratic political boss who controlled the local school-system hiring. Anyone who got a job teaching in the county school system paid a monthly fee to Adair for the privilege. Principals, teachers and school service personnel all paid kickbacks for the jobs they held.

Statewide, this system of payoffs was called the Flower Fund. It was so named because it was said to have been created by the state Democratic Party to collect contributions from party faithful to buy flowers for party members and bigwigs who passed away. In reality, Flower Fund money was used to influence elections and keep Democrats in power—they held a two to one voting advantage and had for many years. Democratic Party honchos controlled jobs in county education, in the state road commission and elsewhere, and individuals had to pay to get and keep their jobs.

In that era, political corruption got so bad in Mingo County that we formed a coalition to try to clean up the local school board. We were successful with our slate of reformers and won the election by an almost two-to-one majority.

In 1960, I ran for mayor of Gilbert again and won. I was elected a second time in 1962, and during my terms in office, I was able to get streetlights installed and establish an effective water system for the town.

I decided not to seek a third term. Instead, I talked the town recorder, Pierce Fox, into running. He was a teacher and a highly regarded individual, and I thought he would be a shoo-in. I advised him to run on a platform of installing new sidewalks in Gilbert because I had seen the positive impact that new sidewalks had made in the nearby community of Oceana. "It will dress the town up," I told him, "and people will be pleased to not have to walk on the highway or in the mud." But we learned that we should have done more homework. None of us had realized that the lawful method of installing sidewalks required the property owners to foot the bill. Poor Pierce got beat three to one.

If you donate to a candidate who is running for political office, other candidates quickly find their way to your door. They want both your money and your perceived influence to help get elected. Elected officials will contact you to help them with a variety of problems. It's surprising sometimes to look up and see "friends" you never knew you had. Once in a while you'll even get a veiled threat, especially if you yourself are confrontational.

I remember in the '60s when Hulett Smith was running for governor against Cecil Underwood. He came to Gilbert to campaign, and I stopped to say hello because I had known him when he headed the state commerce department. "Buck, you're going to help me in this campaign, aren't you?" Hulett asked.

I said, "Hulett, you know I can't help you. Cecil Underwood is my long-time friend and I'm going to support Cecil."

"Don't you have log trucks running up and down the highway?" he asked. The question was odd, and I took it as some kind of threat.

"Yeah, everyday," I answered. "Hulett, you're not trying to intimidate me, are you? Oh no! Oh no!" I shot back, pretending to be afraid. "I'll tell you what," I said. "Those log trucks will be running on the highway long after you're gone from office." I decided then and there to take a stand for the things I believed in politically, and I've tried to do just that. By and large, being active in politics hasn't hurt me. Even that little skirmish with Hulett turned into nothing, and we're good friends today.

I've learned that if you're up front with politicians, even though they may not agree with you, they are usually not vindictive.

People have pitched me to run for statewide office, but I've never seriously considered doing so. Once my friend, Lawson Hamilton, who could be a real jokester, and I made up a story that one of us was going to run for U.S. Senate against Jay Rockefeller. The premise was that we hadn't decided which one of us would do it, only that each of us had the resources to be competitive against Jay and his millions.

I was at a meeting in Charleston with Charlie Jones, Lawson Hamilton and others, when Charlie's secretary came in and said, "Buck, Senator Rockefeller is on the phone, and he wants to speak with you."

I stepped out to take the call from Senator Rockefeller, who was calling from Wyoming, where he had a home. "Now, Buck," he began. "We've been friends a long time, and I know you'll tell me the truth. Are you planning to run against me?"

"Well now, Senator, there have been some suggestions that I should do that, but I certainly haven't made up my mind one way or the other."

"Now Buck, you know that would be the wrong thing to do. I would hope you wouldn't do that." He also wondered aloud if Lawson might be thinking about running, but I was noncommittal about that too.

I went back to the meeting and told Lawson about our conversation. "I bet you'll be getting a call soon, Lawson."

The next night, Lawson got his call, and Rockefeller posed the same question. Lawson gave him the same answer that I did but took the charade a step further by calling Fanny Seiler, a political and gossip columnist for *The Charleston Gazette*, and planting a story with her. Lawson told Fanny that he and I were going to draw straws to see who was going to run against Rockefeller. The Rockefeller camp took our little game seriously for a while, but because neither of us entered the race, the rumor lost traction. I don't know whether the senator ever found out that we were just pulling his leg, but the joke was fun while it lasted.

I think the reason that Jay suffered jokes like this was because he was a "child of privilege" and never seemed to walk in the same shoes as the rest of us. Randy Cline, a Wyoming County native and weekly newspaper publisher, served as Rockefeller's communications secretary. He told the following story about Rockefeller when Jay was secretary of state:

Jay, as he liked to be called, got his first paycheck and was puzzled by it. Addressing one of his assistants, he remarked, "My salary is supposed to be so and so, and this check is less than what it should be."

The assistant cleared his throat and explained, "Well sir, they take out for social security, unemployment tax and other deductions."

"Do they do that for everybody?" Jay asked.

"Yes sir. Everybody."

Apparently, Jay had no idea. Can you imagine that?

When he was governor, Rockefeller called me one day with a proposal to build an addition to the athletic facilities building at West Virginia University to help make the football program more competitive.

I told him that I thought it was a wonderful idea.

Rockefeller asked me, "Will you participate?"

"Sure, I'll participate."

About three or four days later, Rockefeller called again, "Buck, how much are you going to pledge?"

"I hadn't given it much thought, Governor. Do you have to know now?"

"Well, I'd like to know."

"OK, I'll give you a $100,000."

"Fine."

The night the pledge amounts were made public, I noticed that several of us had committed $100,000 each and that Rockefeller had committed $105,000. It appears that he wanted to be sure that he gave more than anyone else.

Stories abound about Rockefeller, who is wealthy by anyone's standards. He apparently never carries pocket money. Instead, he calls upon an aide or a member of his security detail when there is an immediate need for cash.

Don Nehlen, the football coach at WVU for many years, called me one day and said, "I've talked the governor into coming with me to visit a recruit in Ohio, and I want you to come with us because his family is originally from Gilbert." I agreed to go and even offered our plane to take us. I flew to Charleston, picked up the governor and his state police security detail, then to Morgantown to get Nehlen and then on to Ohio.

We met the boy, a fine young man, and his father, whom I knew well. Nehlen made an excellent presentation, and the boy decided on the spot to go to WVU. We were elated. Although he is not a drinker, Nehlen exclaimed, "Does anyone in the house have any whiskey? This calls for a celebration!" The old man brought out some whiskey and all of us had a small congratulatory drink.

On the way back to the airport, we stopped to eat dinner. The governor said, "Dinner's on me."

I thought that his offer was reasonable, since I had furnished the airplane to get us there. We ate our meal, and when it was time to pay the check, Rockefeller fumbled around for a moment, then turned to the state policeman and asked, "Do you have any money with you?" (The story that made the rounds was that he very rarely paid the troopers back. Perhaps an expense account was maintained for reimbursement.)

When Rockefeller became a U.S. Senator, he did not take Randy Cline to Washington, D.C., with him. Randy was content to stay in Mingo County, but we kidded him nevertheless, telling him that he obviously wasn't smart or sophisticated enough to work in a big city.

Randy Cline had the sharpest sense of humor of anyone I've ever met. Once, a customer from England was visiting Gilbert for the first time. We were having lunch, and Randy sat at the table with us.

"Tell me a little about Gilbert," the Englishman said, making well-mannered small talk.

"Well," Randy responded, "Gilbert has three furniture stores, a liquor store, two drug stores, three police officers..."

He ran down the list. "About the only thing we don't have is a town drunk, so we choose up and take turns at that."

Cecil Underwood made his last run for governor in 2000 against U.S Representative Bob Wise. Wise sought my support, but I told him that I was for Underwood. Wise said, "Well, I'm going to win this election, and when I do, I'll come back to see you."

Cecil called me one day interested in knowing the thinking of legendary U.S. Senator Robert C. Byrd. "Buck," he said, "we've heard that Senator Byrd is going to take a hands-off position with regard to the governor's race. Can you confirm with the senator whether the rumor is true or not?" If the rumor turned out to be true, it would have been good news for Underwood, since Senator Byrd's political shadow in the state was immense. I called Senator Byrd, and he went into this long monologue about his high regard for Underwood, how they had served together in the West Virginia House of Delegates 50 years ago and how they had been friends for so long. Finally he said, "I'm not going to do anything to hurt Cecil."

Byrd didn't do anything for a long time, but two weeks before the election, he made a series of appearances all over the state during which he sang the praises of Bob Wise. Many agree that Underwood narrowly lost the election owing to Byrd's last-minute involvement.

After the election, I had a chance to speak with Senator Byrd on another matter, and after we talked through the main subject of conversation, I said to him, "You've always been a truthful man. Why did you tell me that you didn't want to hurt Cecil Underwood, yet you came out in a big way for Wise in the final weeks of the campaign? Many say you are the reason that Cecil lost the race."

"Now Buck," he said, "you know I'm a Democrat, and I've served in Congress with Bob Wise. People came to me and said he was going to lose the election if I didn't get on board. Being a Democratic Party leader, I had to step forward and help."

Senator Byrd tried calling Underwood after our conversation, but Cecil wouldn't take his call.

Bob Wise became governor, and after about three months in office, he called me and said, "I'd like to come and see you." He came to Gilbert. "I told you that I would win and that I would come back to see you, but I'm not going to be vindictive, Buck. I'm not going to put the dogs on you."

I said, "Well, I hope not." And he didn't.

Sometime later, Jim Bunn, who was a big Wise supporter, set up a luncheon at the governor's mansion. He invited a number of people from the business community to share their concerns with the new administration. I was invited but wasn't thrilled to go because the governor had not even begun to do what he had promised during his campaign.

However, Bunn insisted that I attend, and I hesitantly agreed to show up. When it came time to have a fruitful dialogue with the governor, I was surprised to discover that, oddly, everyone in the room was too timid to speak up. You would've thought that Bob Wise was their father—or godfather—and not one person dared to raise any issues with him. Finally, the governor said, "Buck, I haven't heard anything from you."

"Governor," I responded, "I've been listening mostly, but I thought we were invited here to tell you about our problems and to suggest how you might be able to solve them. I know you didn't create these problems. I was hoping, however, that we had a governor who had the guts to stand up and do something about these long-standing issues, but I haven't seen him yet."

You could've heard a pin drop in that room.

Governor Wise said, "I haven't had time, Buck."

"Governor," I answered, "you've been in office for over a year." After our minor standoff, the conversation in the room became more robust and forthright from all sides. A real discussion took place. Sadly, however, nothing much ever came of it.

I've met several presidents including Dwight Eisenhower, Richard Nixon, Gerald Ford, Ronald Reagan, George H. Bush and George W. Bush. Ronald Reagan was very engaging, and I can easily see why he was so popular. In fact, all of the presidents that I've met were more impressive in person than on TV.

I got involved with George W. Bush's presidential campaign in West Virginia and got to know him and his father as a result. Bush became quite unpopular in his second term, but I will tell you, having had the opportunity to know him personally, that he is a man of character, a man of strong will and a man who does not back away from issues that he wants to tackle.

I first met him when he was governor of Texas. He invited me and Tom Potter, another strong Republican from West Virginia, to Austin for a meeting when he was laying groundwork for his first run for president. I sat beside him at the table and listened carefully while people in the room asked him a variety of questions. I asked one myself, "Governor, I'm from

West Virginia, and I'm in the coal business. We're all very anxious to find out how you would stand on the issue of coal."

He said, "Now, Buck, you know I've been in the oil business, so I'm for oil and I'm for coal. But, I've got to play it down. Al Gore will hammer me if I come out strongly for it because he's an environmentalist. I can't come out and say that I'm willing to do this for coal and I'm going to do this for oil because he'll use it against me. But, you rest assured, I'm on your side."

I served as the West Virginia finance chairman for the Bush campaign in the 2000 election. The race was a squeaker, and he was finally declared the winner after much turmoil and vote recounting in Florida. Critical, too, was the fact that he won West Virginia and its electoral delegates, which was something a Republican presidential candidate hadn't done since Ronald Reagan in 1984. Had he not won West Virginia winning Florida would have meant nothing. I had the pleasure to vote in the Electoral College and to cast the vote that elected him President of the United States.

Having supported the President the way I did meant that I was invited to certain presidential social functions. On one occasion, President Bush invited Hallie and me to attend a private gathering in Cincinnati, a fundraiser for the Ohio Republican congressional delegation. I was pleased to attend because I've learned that it's never routine to be in any social situation with the President of the United States. Such events are complicated affairs, considering all the preparations, security measures and scheduling that takes place.

For attendees, getting to the event early is important, since the Secret Service closes the airport about an hour before the president is scheduled to land. Arriving early typically means that passing through security is less arduous, and the early bird has time to casually meet and talk with interesting people in usually beautiful surroundings.

At this event, our hosts had set up a very substantial gleaming-white, air-conditioned tent for the dinner party. The weather that evening was hot, but you'd never have known it as we stood inside the lavish, cool tent. When Hallie and I got our nametags, which also indicated where we were to be seated, we noticed the initials HT on them and wondered what it meant. The air conditioning inside the tent was so effective that Hallie and I both got a little cold, so we walked out onto the perfectly manicured lawn and found a couple of chairs under a large tree.

I saw a familiar face: it was Mercer Reynolds, Bush's finance chairman for both of his presidential campaigns. Mercer and I had become pretty decent friends because we're both interested in a program for abused children and families, something we had worked together on for several years before our mutual involvement with the Bush campaign. Mercer walked over to us and smiled, "Buck, could I get you and Hallie a glass of wine or something?"

"Yes, thank you."

He returned with two glasses of Chardonnay.

"Mercer," I said, "Help me out with something. On our nametags, there's this designation HT. Do you know what that means?"

"HT stands for head table," Mercer answered. "You and Hallie will be sitting with the President at dinner." The evening was becoming more and more interesting.

"Will Carl Lindner be here tonight?" I asked Mercer. Carl Lindner was someone I had wanted to meet for sometime.

Among other things, he was the majority stock owner in Provident Bank and American Financial Group, and at the time, he was also a co-owner of the Cincinnati Reds. His attendance at the gathering excited me greatly because I had never met a billionaire. There aren't many billionaires around, so the prospect of meeting one was something very special.

"I know Carl is supposed to be here this evening," Mercer said.

"I've never met him," I responded, "but I'd certainly like to."

"When he gets here," Mercer promised, "I'll introduce you."

I took another sip of wine and noticed that the crowd of people around the tent was growing steadily. A dark blue Rolls Royce convertible pulled up. The driver stayed behind the wheel, and two men stepped out. It seemed from the younger one's sturdy physique and demeanor that he was a bodyguard for the other, an older, distinguished-looking gentleman, perhaps 75 years old, about five feet nine inches tall and immaculately dressed in a well-tailored light-brown suit. I was pretty certain that this was Carl Lindner.

At about the same time, from another direction, the President entered the tent and began greeting guests. Before dinner, the President gave every single person in attendance a little personal time as well as having a picture taken together. When the President saw me, he greeted me with a hearty "Big Buck," the nickname he had given me when we first met years earlier in Texas. (Several people have asked me why the President calls me "Big Buck," and I just don't know. Every time we've met, that's how he's greeted me. He's been so warm and friendly that I've always felt pretty good about it.)

"Hello, Mr. President."

Hallie, President Bush and I made small talk for a minute

or two while a photographer took our picture. After a few minutes of greetings, small talk and photographs, the guests started taking their seats. We were shown to the head table where we were seated in the middle of 12 other people. Mr. Lindner took a seat directly across from me and an empty chair sat to his left. In the other chairs sat some of the wealthiest and most impressive big contributors in Ohio. I struck up an informal conversation with Mr. Lindner, who was friendly, although fairly reserved. All of those around the table were casually getting acquainted when the President came up and took the empty seat beside Mr. Lindner. He looked directly across the table at Hallie and me and said, "Big Buck, you're in high cotton tonight here at the head table!"

He was in a great mood, smiling and casual. President Bush is one of the most likeable people I've ever met. His personality is much warmer and charming in person than what people see on television, and he seemed to be in an especially good mood that evening. With the President now seated, the guests fell silent out of respect. The protocol in such situations is to give deference to the president who is the guest of honor.

The President looked around, nodded at me and asked, "Folks, have you met this fellow here yet?" There was a brief pause. "Then let me introduce you. This is Buck Harless. He's probably one of the men most responsible for me being President." All eyes turned to me, and I have never been more surprised or more aware of being the focus of attention in my life.

"Mr. President," I responded, "aren't you exaggerating a little bit?" I immediately felt a tinge of embarrassment for what I had said in reply.

The President only smiled; he didn't say a word.

I was happy when the conversation finally turned to other

topics, yet uncomfortable that I had not responded more appropriately. Still, it was flattering for the President to praise me in such a way. Moments later I was formally introduced to Mr. Lindner by the President himself.

I recall another memorable evening with the President when Hallie and I were invited to a social function at the White House, a dinner to honor Nobel Prize winners. While we were waiting at the White House gate for entry to the affair, a limousine pulled up and out stepped Henry Kissinger. He nodded hello to me as he got out of the car, and a few moments later, I walked over and introduced myself.

"Mr. Kissinger, I'm James Harless from West Virginia, and this is my wife, Hallie. I've always been an admirer of yours." While we waited to be escorted into the White House, Kissinger, Hallie and I had a very pleasant conversation.

It was quite an evening. For the life of me, I couldn't understand why the President decided to invite Hallie and me to a function with such sophisticated intellectuals, professors and the like. Hallie even asked President Bush, "Mr. President, why are we here?"

The President smiled and asked her what she meant.

"Why are we here with such distinguished, important Americans?" Hallie asked.

President Bush took her arm and said simply, "Because you're my friends."

Still, I was puzzled as to why we were included in a group of extraordinarily brilliant people, some of whom were strange-looking characters with uncombed hair and scruffy-looking suits. I really felt out of place. I sat beside a Laureate and his wife who turned to me and asked, "What did you get your Laureate for?"

I explained to her that I was just a guest, but I almost told her "for sawmilling."

It was an altogether incongruous evening, but ultimately a real honor and one of the most fascinating nights of my life. I've learned that being invited to the White House can place you among the most interesting people.

In 2006, while President Bush was serving his final term, U.S. Senator Robert C. Byrd ran for re-election. I had known the senator for many years and considered him a good friend. He did many good things for West Virginia from his senate post, and I held him in high regard and voted for him.

I attended the premiere of a documentary about Senator Byrd at the Clay Center in Charleston and had just entered the building when Anne Barth, the senator's right-hand lady, approached me. "Please come with me, Mr. Harless. The senator wants to speak with you." She led me down a hallway to a small, private room where Senator Byrd sat.

"Buck, good to see you," he got up and hugged me. "Buck," he said, "I'm happy that you've come today. I'm so glad to see you." The previous week he had called wanting me to serve on his re-election finance committee, but I had declined remembering how he had helped defeat Cecil Underwood in the 2000 governor's race. That night he was still after me to support his candidacy. "Now Buck, you told me that you wouldn't serve on my finance committee, but I want you to be for me. And I want you to donate too."

"Senator, I'll have to think about that."

"Now Buck, you said that before." But he kept on, "I want you to be for me. I want you to be for me. I want you to be for me." Three times he said it.

"Okay, I'll vote for you," I answered.

"Will you help me raise money?"

"I won't do that, but I will vote for you." And I did.

Senator Byrd was an early critic of President Bush's incursion into Iraq, and he was probably the President's most ardent critic on the subject. When the White House heard of my promise to vote for Senator Byrd, I received a call from a campaign underling who implied that this might affect my relationship with the president. For a short time, his admonition appeared to be true. I had very few dealings with the White House, although Karl Rove continued to take my calls while he still worked there.

It turned out that the President maintained our friendship. Since the election, I've been to the White House for dinner and also have spent time in the Oval Office, discussing issues with the President. There were 12 of us at a White House dinner, which was hosted by the President and First Lady. The conversations covered many topics. The President was quite frank in his discussions, and also about certain mistakes he believed he had made while in office. He stated that he had come to Washington with certain principles that he had lived by and that he'd be going back to Texas with those same principles. At the Oval Office meeting, I took Hallie and some friends with me to meet the President. They included my minister, Chris Turner, and his wife, Amy; my doctor, Billy Mullen, and his wife, Shari; Gary White and his wife, Jo Ann; and my daughter, Judy. The President was very informal with our group. To Reverend Turner he said, "You know for a time, Preacher, I was pretty bad to drink, but I quit when I started seeing ghosts." He asked Dr. Mullen about his medical specialty.

Dr. Mullen, excited to be talking with the President in the Oval Office, answered, "I'm Buck's doctor." (We kid him about his response to this day.)

I was told before the meeting that it was scheduled to last about 15 minutes. Instead, the meeting lasted an hour, and our conversation covered a wide variety of subjects. When he was asked about the incoming president, the only thing George Bush said was, "I think he will learn, when he sits down in this chair, that things will not be as easy as he anticipated. I'm sure that any incoming president will find that to be true."

For all of us who attended that meeting with the President, it will be an enduring memory.

It is important to note that even though I have worked with chief executives of the state and of the nation, during their campaigns and while they were in office, there is one thing I want to state very clearly: never once have I sought special treatment for myself from anyone in political office at any level for any reason.

Chapter Thirteen

I have always had the tendency to drive fast: some say too fast for my own good. During my bad drinking days, my tendency to speed was much worse. I recall once racing a fellow over at Iaeger, and it wasn't the smartest thing I ever did. We were in a club on the other side of Johnny Cake Mountain and were bragging about who had the faster car. In a barroom setting, bragging can quickly lead to betting, and the next thing you know he and I were making a rather substantial wager on who had the faster car.

We left the bar and headed out to race to the top of the mountain. Beyond being foolish to race in the first place, I was very foolish in two additional ways. First, the right front tire on my Oldsmobile convertible was low on air, and I discounted that fact. Second, when we lined our cars up at the starting point, a rear wheel of my car rested on the shoulder, not on the highway. My challenger did better than I; he lined up his car completely on the highway. When we took off, his car shot forward, and my car careened left and right, its tires spinning wildly. When we reached a sharp curve at the foot of the mountain, I was not yet firmly in control of my car, and I knew I was in trouble. The tire with low air helped to throw the car completely out of control in that curve, and we skidded off the highway and into a cliff. I say we because my brother, Bud, was with me in the car, proving that he was just as silly as I.

When we wrecked, I was thrown from the car, and Bud was knocked out. Our injuries did not require hospitalization, however. I suffered a cut on my lip and my elbow hurt like the dickens, but nothing more. Bud regained consciousness quickly. My good-looking yellow Oldsmobile convertible got the worst of it: it caught fire and burned up before our eyes.

We were so thoughtless; we both could have died that day. I could have been dead a long time ago. Maybe I'm a little like a cat with nine lives.

In the late '50s, I was hurrying back to Gilbert from Gary, where I did a lot of business with U.S. Steel. When I say that I was hurrying, I mean that I was driving fast but not recklessly. There's a difference between fast and reckless, at least in my mind. At Roderfield, I saw a fellow with crutches hitchhiking, so I stopped and gave him a ride.

"Where are you headed?" I asked.

"I'm going to Huntington," he answered.

"Well," I said, "I can get you about 18 miles closer to your destination."

"Fine."

I sped down the highway, a little heavy on the accelerator, and a short time later, we entered the town of Iaeger.

"You see that filling station down there on the left?" my passenger asked.

"Yeah."

"Let me out right there."

I quickly realized that I might have scared him with my

driving. "Now, I can still take you farther down the highway."

"No, no. Let me out right there."

I stopped at the gas station, got his crutches from the back seat and helped him out of the car. As I started to pull away, he said, "Mister, you can go from here to your house in 10 minutes, and I don't give a damn where you live."

To give you an idea of how life has changed, let me share this: A year or two ago, I was involved in an unusual wreck, and I hardly had to do a thing. I was coming off of U.S. Route 119 onto state highway 44 at a traffic light in Logan. I approached the traffic light behind a female driver just as the light was turning orange. She kept moving as if she was going on through the light, but at the last instant, she stopped abruptly. Well, my car bumped her rear bumper just a little bit. Seeing what I had done, I decided that I should back up just a little to see if I had damaged her car. I put my car in reverse and immediately backed into a small red sports car that had been waiting at the light behind me. Man, the sports car driver was so upset. "What in the hell is wrong with you?"

"Well, I bumped into this lady and was backing up to see if I'd harmed her car."

"Look what you did!" He just kept raising hell.

"Well, I can't see that I did any damage to your car."

He carefully inspected his vehicle and finally said, "Well, I guess it's alright."

Two accidents in a matter of seconds; I couldn't have done it any quicker if I had tried. Still, I was relieved that no harm was done.

Growing up, I never imagined in my wildest dreams that I would travel very far beyond the hills of West Virginia, even though reading books fueled my desire to experience other peoples and their cultures firsthand. As a child, I considered owning an automobile to be the mark of real success. The thought of owning an airplane was pure fantasy, and traveling in my own aircraft to far away countries would have been delusional. But I've learned that one must never fail to dream.

I've been able to travel widely: to every state except North and South Dakota; every province in Canada; Cuba, Haiti and Puerto Rico; Guatemala, El Salvador, Panama, Costa Rica and Ecuador; every country in South America except for Suriname and French Guiana; Iceland, Greenland, Ireland, England, France, Germany, Portugal, Spain, Italy and Gibraltar; Australia, New Zealand, China, Japan; and maybe some others that I've overlooked.

Over the years, I've owned a number of airplanes. The first was a single-engine Cessna, and the second was a twin-engine Beechcraft Baron. A fellow named Leo Nehrt, a farm boy from Indiana, flew for me in the early days. I once let Leo borrow the Baron during the Christmas holidays so he could visit his family, and he crashed it attempting to land. Thankfully, no one was hurt. He called me with the news and an additional problem. How, he wondered, was he going to get back to West Virginia? I thought the way he presented his quandary was rather amusing, and how he got back to West Virginia was clearly his problem to solve. I bought another Baron and then a Beechcraft King Air B90 twin turboprop. We later bought a Cessna Citation II and finally a Citation III. With each aircraft purchase, we were able to increase comfort, speed and range.

The Citation III seats eight passengers, cruises at 500 mph and has a range of 1,000 miles. It's an aircraft that can take you all over the world provided you have a reasonable place to land and take off.

Charles W. "Cotton" McGlothlin became my pilot during the Baron era, and he held that position for 28 years. Besides being an exceptionally good pilot, he also was reliable and diligent. I don't recall him ever being late or missing a flight.

Most of Cotton's flying was to and from South America, and I always felt safe with him at the controls. During Cotton's tenure as our pilot, he logged an enormous number of miles without incident, but I recall a couple of heart-thumping moments. Once we were flying into Mobile in terrible weather and a very low ceiling. Fred Shewey was in a back seat and I was riding co-pilot. We were relying on instruments to guide our landing, and we couldn't see a thing in front of us except for rain on the windshield and fuzzy, gray clouds. With such a low ceiling, we weren't expecting to see the ground or the runway until seconds before touchdown. Each pilot had his own altimeter, and when we were on final approach, I noticed that Cotton's altimeter reading was 100 feet higher than mine. Concerned, I mentioned the discrepancy to him. Cotton, intent on reading his instruments and controlling the glide, replied that he thought his altimeter was correct. About that time, I was barely able to glimpse a kid fishing at the edge of an ill-defined body of water, and an instant later, I saw a rock cliff straight ahead and instinctively pulled back on the controls to regain altitude and avoid catastrophe. We had been 100 feet lower than we thought and had very nearly crashed. It was a close call and I'm lucky to be able to tell you the story.

Another time we were in Paraguay, South America, where we had flown to collect money owed to us by a company that had not delivered the lumber that it had contractually promised. On our return, we flew north to Paraguay's capitol city of Asunción. Our next leg took us to Santa Cruz, Bolivia. From there we had a long flight over long stretches of jungle back to Manaus, Brazil. It was almost dark when I noticed that Cotton seemed to be getting a little nervous. When you see your pilot becoming nervous, you start paying close attention and become uneasy yourself.

"Cotton," I asked, quickly focusing on the most frightening subject to come to mind, "how much fuel do we have?"

"I think we have enough."

"Thinking," I said, "is not good enough for me. I certainly hope you're right."

By the time we touched down, we had only 15 minutes of fuel remaining. We didn't say much to each other after landing, but we were greatly relieved.

Back in the States, I told my brother, Fred, about the experience. "You know, Buck," he said, "if you had crashed, they never would have found you."

"Fred," I answered, "they wouldn't even have looked for us."

I recall flying with Cotton to a village south of our operation to purchase lumber. We landed at a little airstrip and pulled up to the terminal, which was nothing more than a little shack. Out of the shack to our surprise, came four uniformed individuals carrying automatic weapons. They yanked Cotton, who was only five feet eight inches tall and 140 pounds, out of the airplane and told me to stay put. They took

Cotton into the shack, and I waited at the plane for over an hour, growing all the more concerned as each minute slowly passed in the hot Brazilian sun. Finally, Cotton emerged looking haggard and beat, explaining that he had been obligated to convince the soldiers that we were not terrorists intent on overthrowing the military government. Eventually, he said, they accepted his explanation that we were there to purchase mahogany lumber from a local mill.

On a similar trip, we had to decide, while circling a dirt airstrip, whether to attempt a landing because the landing area appeared to be muddy. Cotton, ever the optimist, opined that it would probably be OK, while I, occasionally gullible, concluded that he was probably right.

When we touched down, we immediately sank into heavy mud and the plane came to a sudden halt. While landing was no big problem—except for sinking—taking off was going to be impossible. So we decided to vacation for a few days in the middle of nowhere, while the world around us dried out.

Local accommodations proved neither inviting nor pleasant, but we made do sleeping on the floor of a rickety establishment that gamely called itself a hotel. Our security guard, graciously provided by our hosts, slept on a hammock in the stairwell. The first night, unable to sleep, I got up, looked around and noticed that our peacefully snoring guard was so thoroughly covered with mosquitoes that it was difficult to discern his human form.

Over the course of our three-day stay, locals assisted us in pulling our plane to dry ground and the sun baked enough of the runway to allow for a safe takeoff. We bought some nice mahogany too.

I visited with Cotton not long ago in Titusville, Florida, where he moved after retirement. He lives alone now, having lost his wife about three years ago. He's on dialysis and his health is deteriorating. We had a good visit and swapped a number of stories about our 28 years together. I believe fate caused our paths to cross and for him to become my pilot.

Our current fixed-wing pilots, Bill Harvey and John Huffman, are the ones who have flown us to Europe and elsewhere. Both Bill and John are two fine young men, good Christians and excellent pilots, who are dedicated in their jobs. I feel very comfortable when I fly with them, and we've flown a good portion of the world together.

The first helicopter I bought was a Hughes 200, a gasoline-powered turbocharged two-seater that I flew myself. I made the purchase on the condition that the company I bought it from would also provide my training, so a pilot came to Gilbert to teach me how to fly the thing. One Saturday morning, I said to him, "Let's work all day, so we can cover everything, and you can turn me loose on this thing."

He said, "OK, let's fly to Prestonsburg, Kentucky." We flew there and I got the helicopter fueled up for the return trip, while he spent his time talking to another fellow I didn't know.

I thought he was wasting good training time, so I said, "Let's get on with the training."

He responded, "I've got to go to Lexington, and this fellow here is going to take me."

"But…" I protested, knowing full well that I was not ready to fly alone.

"Oh, you'll do fine. Gotta go." And he left just like that.

On my solo back to Gilbert, I heard things inside that helicopter I had never heard before and imagined that it was falling apart. However, those fictitious gremlins did not get the best of me, and I made it back without incident.

Two days later, I had to go to Harlan, Kentucky. I made the trip by myself in my new helicopter, which continued to make sounds that concerned me. I obviously spent too much time listening and not enough time navigating. I flew over a little town but couldn't identify it, and I promptly realized I was lost.

There was little in the way of landmarks, just steep mountains and an open field. Luckily, I spied what seemed to be a pipeline crew working in the field below and decided to land and verify my location to get reoriented. The crew seemed surprised to see a helicopter land nearby, the pilot leave the aircraft with its engine still running and ask them a simple question, "Can any of you tell me the name of the little town back there?"

They told me its name, and I thanked them for their assistance, climbed back into the helicopter and flew away. All the time, the pipeline crew watched me with mute curiosity. I was grateful to have discovered them, and after my departure, I bet they made a wisecrack or two about my dropping in on them.

Later I purchased a Bell Jet Ranger, a very popular helicopter that was flown by many businesses and by the U.S. Army and Air Force in modified versions. I suggested to Cotton and others that they learn to fly it, but no one warmed to the suggestion. So I hired a pilot to fly the Jet Ranger.

My first Jet Ranger pilot was Tom Renison, and he flew for me for about three years. He's now living in Florida. He came all that way to help me celebrate my 90th birthday at a party in Charleston, the first time I had seen him since he left many years ago.

The second pilot was Davey Crocket, a young man from Davy in nearby McDowell County. He turned out to be very unreliable, and I had to discharge him because I couldn't depend on him.

Gene Jones was my third pilot. Gene was a Vietnam veteran, who had flown in all kinds of weather and circumstances. He was an excellent pilot and a first-rate travel companion. I recall one morning we were loading up to fly somewhere. As I buckled myself up in the front passenger seat, Gene said, "Mr. Harless, today's my anniversary!"

"Congratulations," I answered, thinking he was referring to his and his wife's wedding anniversary. "Tell Mary Lou that I send sincere congratulations to her also."

"Oh," he said, "not that kind of anniversary. Today marks 25 years that I've been flying helicopters for you."

It sure didn't seem that long.

Gene was not only an outstanding pilot but also a good individual, who was very reliable. He chose to live in Princeton and commuted to Gilbert, a more than 90-minute drive one way. Occasionally, I'd let him take the helicopter home with him, mainly if we had a late night or were going to have an early morning.

Just a few years ago, Gene flew Gary White to Tennessee. After landing, Gary and Gene exited the still-running aircraft, and Gary headed for the flight terminal, while Gene gathered up Gary's luggage. In a freak accident that no one fully understands, the helicopter's main-rotor blade struck Gene in the head, killing him instantly.

It was a particularly sad incident for everyone because Gene was a dear friend, so good-natured and pleasant. Of course, his wife, Mary Lou, was grief stricken.

Gene was such a good fellow. The accident was a tragic end to a life well lived.

Early in President George W. Bush's first term, he appointed me a trustee of the U.S. Air Force Academy in Colorado Springs, Colorado. As a result of that appointment, I had the good fortune to meet General Robert H. "Doc" Foglesong, a four-star U.S. Air Force general, who was born in nearby Chattaroy in Mingo County. General Fogelsong holds three degrees in chemical engineering from West Virginia University. He received his bachelor's degree in 1968 and his Ph.D. in 1971, so you can see that he is able to apply himself to the task at hand. While at WVU, he received only one grade of B, and that was from his future wife, Mary, an instructor who apparently held him to exceedingly high standards. He had an impressive air force career as a pilot and commander, and retired in February 2006 as Commander of U.S. Air Forces Europe.

In 2004, General Fogelsong was visiting his mother, who still lived in Chattaroy. He stopped by to see me and invited me and Hallie to visit him at U.S. Air Forces Europe (USAFE) Headquarters at Ramstein Air Base in Germany. Of course, we were happy to accept his invitation and excited to visit with him and his wife.

When we set out on our trip to Germany, we flew first to Gander, Newfoundland, and then to Keflavik, Iceland. General Fogelsong had made arrangements for us to stay at the air base at the Keflavik Naval Air Station. (The air force base there was a tenant organization commanded by USAFE.) The general also had Colonel Richard Weathers, his finance officer at USAFE, to meet us in Iceland. It was clear that General Fogelsong wanted us to be treated well because Colonel Weathers made sure that we had the best hospitality and service. We spent a delightful night at Keflavik and had a fine dinner and good conversation with the officers stationed there.

The next day we flew to England to refuel and then on to Ramstein Air Base, the largest U.S. Air Force base in Europe. With about 53,000 people working there, it serves as the main transportation hub for medical support and for all air mobility in Europe.

After we touched down in the rain at Ramstein and began to taxi, a black BMW pulled in front of our plane. Momentarily, a raised arm appeared from the driver's window motioning us to follow the car. It was General Fogelsong. I told our pilot, John Huffman, that I bet he had never been escorted to a ramp by a four-star general. We loaded our luggage into the BMW and proceeded to the general's home on the base, where we were shown to the guesthouse, which provided very comfortable accommodations.

The next morning, I went with the general to his office. Behind his desk on the wall, was a sign that read "Welcome to Ramstein Air Base Buck and Hallie." To prove that this is a small world, General Fogelsong invited two non-commissioned officers, Margaret Akers Horton and Steve Collins to have lunch with us. Margaret is the daughter of Ray Akers, who worked for us at Hampden Coal Company, and Steve is the grandson of a Collins boy from Matewan whom I played football and basketball against in high school. Both were stationed at the air base.

Being a four-star general places an individual at the top of the heap. As General Fogelsong's guest, I was privy to the respect and deference given to him and his status, something that General Fogelsong wore very well.

One morning, I left our guesthouse without a jacket, but it turned out to be cooler than I'd thought. When I got to his office, the general gave me one of his jackets to wear, one with four stars emblazoned on it. Throughout the day, General Fogelsong sometimes would be called away to attend to important matters, and while on my own and wearing the general's jacket, I was saluted more than once, obviously by those who only saw the four stars. Otherwise, they would have concluded that I was oldest general they had ever come across.

On a Sunday during our visit, Mary suggested that we have dinner at an old castle on the Rhine River. For security reasons, the general was not permitted to travel in a car alone beyond the base. In those circumstances, he traveled with a driver/bodyguard. So it was that evening with the general and I in the back seat, and Mary and Hallie in another car altogether. We had a lovely dinner at the castle, which was hundreds of years old.

On Monday afternoon, I was sitting in the general's office along with a colonel. The three of us were talking about world affairs, and I was asking about the mission of the base and its importance to U.S. and world security. At one point, I mentioned that we were planning to leave the next morning, and all of a sudden the general said, "Colonel, let's have a party for

Buck and Hallie this evening at the officers' club."

"Well, sir," the colonel hesitated, "this is Monday, and the officers' club is closed."

Without batting an eye, the general said, "Let's open it." In short order they did, and we had a wonderful evening. The mayor attended; and even an orchestra played.

We left the next morning and continued our journey to Paris and other points. It was one of the most memorable trips of the many that I've taken throughout the world. We were treated like royalty by the general and Mary, and I was very happy to break bread with young people who were serving our country so far away from their Mingo County home.

Chapter Fourteen

During the 1970s and '80s, I spent a considerable amount of time in Morgantown working with West Virginia University when I served as chairman to the Board of Advisors to the President. In addition, I was chairman of the board of the West Virginia University Foundation. Being chairman of both entities gave me a unique perspective, and I believe no one has served in those dual capacities before or since.

Lysander Dudley was the executive director of the WVU Foundation at the time. Lysander could be a very colorful, likeable fellow, and he could also be a bear. He was a very good friend of Arch Moore, Jr., who served three terms as West Virginia governor. Lysander had a strong interest in the WVU Marching Band, and many at the university believed that Lysander's interest in the band was greater than his interest in supporting academics. Besides being colorful, he had a great sense of self importance, and his style and method of operation created problems within and beyond the university, but especially among the deans and the administration. His manner also eroded the foundation's ability to raise money for the university.

WVU President Gene Budig called me one day with bad news. "Buck," he said, "I have a revolt on my hands, and I need you to come up here and talk to the deans. They are terribly upset with Lysander."

I went to Morgantown and attended a meeting that Budig had set up with the deans, and I listened to a surprising litany of complaints concerning Lysander's lack of cooperation and respect toward them. Of the 16 deans in attendance that day, all but one spoke in a very incensed manner. I was surprised by the anger and passion in their voices, and I saw then and there that we had a very serious problem. The gist of their pleadings was that something had to be done, or they would have nothing to do with Lysander or the foundation. The foundation's mission was to support the university, and it was clear that Lysander had lost his sense of mission. No foundation can be an effective fund-raiser if potential benefactors know of a serious rift within the university.

I came home and after some thought, gave Lysander a call. "Lysander, I'm wearing myself out coming to Morgantown so frequently. I need to speak with you in person, but I want you to do the traveling this time. Take the foundation's plane and fly down to Williamson, and we can meet in Brooks Lawson's office." Brooks was a member of the foundation's board of directors, and I wanted him to hear what I had learned from the deans, as well as to listen to Lysander's response.

Lysander made the flight to Williamson for the meeting, and I related some of the comments that I had heard from the deans and summed up by saying, "Lysander, you are going to have to change!"

Lysander responded, "Look, I'm in my 50s and I'm too old to change now."

"Well then, we certainly have a problem. If you don't change, you're not going to be successful raising money for the foundation and the university. You're taking a path that has serious, negative consequences, and you are failing both the foundation and the university."

Lysander held his ground and did not change his ways. Tension grew between him and the deans, who were considering suing him, ready to claim that he had misappropriated funds. In the midst of all of this, Gene Budig left WVU to become chancellor of the University of Kansas, and I was asked to chair a search committee to find a new president for WVU.

All the while, Lysander continued his practice of antagonizing the deans and the administration. Gordon Gee, the dean of the WVU Law School and John Fisher, an associate of Gee's, met with Lysander to propose ways to raise funds for the law school. Lysander told Dean Gee that his ideas were crazy, and the conversation became rather heated. "You spend enough time around here," warned Lysander, "and you'll discover who really runs this place."

It became apparent to me that Lysander had to go. I had given him the opportunity to change his behavior, but he had refused. Indeed, he continued to run roughshod over the people he was supposed to serve. Keeping in mind that the board foundation was weighted heavily with members handpicked by Lysander and knowing that he was a consummate politician with the support of the state's governor, it became evident that to affect his ouster would require a swift surgical strike. I learned that Lysander's son was to be married in Boise, Idaho, and that Lysander would be out of state for a few days, allowing me an opportunity to speak freely with the foundation board members about the gravity of the situation.

In my capacity as chairman of the board of the foundation, I called a meeting of the board, and most members attended by telephone. I shared the litany of complaints voiced by the deans and related Lysander's unwillingness to change. I recommended that we ask Lysander to resign, even though I was uncertain that the board would do so. After much discussion, the board agreed with me, and we formally asked for his resignation.

Lysander left the position soon after, and perhaps to his surprise, Gordon Gee became the next president of WVU. We sought a new leader for the foundation, one with the diplomatic and cooperative skills that Lysander lacked. The foundation's endowment began to grow, and a new commitment of cooperation and support was forged between the foundation and the university.

Success and power mean nothing—and can cause great harm—without humility and a basic understanding that we are together in life, and we succeed at endeavors together better than any one of us can do alone.

Gordon Gee proved to be an excellent leader of WVU. Currently, he is the president of The Ohio State University, and a short time ago, *Time* magazine placed him at the top of its list of "The 10 Best College Presidents." Gordon invited Hallie and me, along with John Fisher and his wife, Susie, to spend the weekend and to attend the Wisconsin-Ohio State football game. At the boosters' luncheon prior to the game, we sat with John Glenn, the famed astronaut and former U.S. Senator from Ohio. I told Senator Glenn that my only claim to fame was to chair the search committee that hired Gordon Gee for his first university presidency.

I began adult life with only a high school diploma, and I am very fortunate to have received honorary degrees from West Virginia University, Marshall University, Concord University, Stillman College, Pikeville College and the University of

Charleston. However, part of me still wishes that I could have been a real college student.

I am very proud to have received each honorary degree, and I recall vividly the moments and the people involved. When I received the Marshall University honorary doctorate, U.S. Senator Jennings Randolph was also honored. When we were putting on our robes before the ceremony, Sen. Randolph asked Marshall University President Robert B. Hayes if he could say a few words during the ceremony, a request that did not follow the planned program. Given that it was a U.S. Senator making the request, President Hayes could not refuse.

Instead of a few words, Sen. Randolph, well-known for his long-windedness, spoke for a full 15 minutes. As he went on, people shifted nervously in their seats. On and on he went, and as I sat there, I remembered a story about Senator Randolph that had made the rounds. It seems that the Senator and his wife attended a function where he was a speaker. Afterwards on their way home, Senator Randolph asked his wife how he had done with his speech. "Oh, Jennings," she answered sweetly, "you did exceptionally well. But you missed two or three occasions where you had a wonderful opportunity to stop the talk."

I have smoked since I was 18 years old. At my last physical, the doctor remarked that my lungs were in pretty good shape given the abuse they had received from cigarettes. I wish I had never taken up smoking. I've quit on a number of occasions, but they always seem to find their way back into my life. I was in the hospital not too long ago and could not breathe very well and that about fixed me—I've always had a fear of smothering to death. My greatest attraction to cigarettes is when I have a drink before dinner; that's when I really miss smoking. A scotch almost begs for a cigarette to go with it. I want to give up smoking, and I hope I can. I do not want to have to fight for my breath.

Since I mentioned alcohol, I should point out that I enjoy a drink, particularly before dinner. Over the years, scotch has been my preference. Johnny Walker Blue Label is my choice, although it is too expensive, so I drink Johnny Walker Black. A drink or two is my limit. I'm happy to stop there and go no further.

I've never thought that I was an exceptionally smart businessman, but I believe that I have the gift of recognizing opportunities when they arise. I'm a firm believer that we are preordained to find the opportunities that best suit our purpose; I've always believed that. I think it is up to each individual, however, to succeed with the opportunities presented. I don't know that I was predestined to succeed in business, but I think I was predestined to go into business. That's something that I always wanted. I think we're all predestined to find a vocation. It may be cleaning septic tanks or practicing medicine, but whatever we do, we should work at it and try to do it honorably.

Even the prospect of a one-third interest in that original "peckerwood" sawmill, I saw as opportunity. Perhaps my partners were looking to get out of a shaky investment, but I grasped the opportunity and ran with it asking myself, Now that you've got this chance, what are you going do with it? The answer is that I worked my butt off trying to succeed. Of course that daily struggle was the beginning of International Industries, Inc. The old saying "The harder you work, the luckier you get" really applies, and things have worked out pretty well for me in business.

I've been an optimist throughout my life, and I have faith that bad situations eventually will turn out for the better. I've made a number of mistakes and have been prone to follow the adage "The Lord helps those who help themselves." With smaller problems, I have not sought the Lord's wisdom. Instead of placing my problems in the Lord's hands, I've always been egotistical enough to think that I could solve them myself without His help. There have been occasions when I was overwhelmed with a problem, and I've gotten on my knees and earnestly sought His guidance. I do conclude, however, that more humility and less confidence in myself would have given me a purer Christian attitude.

I've always thought that the Lord gave me certain abilities and that He had some reason for putting me in situations that required me to use my abilities and skills. I've always believed that He led me to something for a purpose, and I think my life almost proves that. It's very clear to me anyway. I hope He thinks that I meant well and that He has excused and forgiven me for my failings, but I don't know. I believe that I could have expressed my faith more humbly.

I'm getting on in years, but I have no desire to retire. To be active and to stay engaged is what really keeps me going. I've learned that to "keep on trying" just may be one of the keys to having lived a long life. Of course, it's clear to me that I have to maintain good health in order to stay active. Frankly I don't know what I'd do if I didn't have any work to perform. It's not always easy to pull myself out of bed in the morning, and life isn't altogether rosy. People look at me and say that I've got it made, but I have problems too.

I've been asked many times why I choose to remain in Gilbert, as if business success dictates that I should live in some metropolitan palace behind a gated entrance. The answer is that I just happen to be a small-town person, and I like to be near my friends. I like the people here in Gilbert, and I like it that the kids here call me Buck. I would never be comfortable in the hustle and bustle of a big city, and I don't relish the thought of driving two hours to work in the morning and then two hours to get home at night, like many commuters do. I do not wish to attend church in an enormous cathedral because I like a small church. I like the little church that I attend. I like the big cities for three or four days at time. I go to New York; I've been trapped in gridlock. I visit Los Angeles; I've driven in 12-lane freeways at 80 miles an hour. Big cities have a lot to offer, but they take a lot out of you at the same time. Gilbert has a lot to give. The mountains and my friends strengthen my soul. They keep me real.

My son, Larry, who was 13 at the time, was spending the summer break at home after his first year at the Greenbrier

Military Academy. I came in from work one evening and found him sitting on the porch looking down in the dumps.

"Son," I asked, "are you OK?"

"Daddy," he complained, "there's just nothing for kids to do around here."

"Oh, son, there are several kids you can play with."

"But what are we going to do? When I grow up and make money, I'm going to build a place in Gilbert for kids to play and have a good time."

After Larry died, his mother and I recalled his statement from childhood and decided to build a community center in Gilbert in his memory. I visited a number of community centers and studied their design and operation. The resulting Larry Joe Harless Community Center (LJHCC) has been a wonderful addition to the community in number of ways.

It has an Olympic-size swimming pool, a gymnasium with a running track, an exercise facility, meeting rooms and banquet facilities. In the beginning, it had three motion picture theaters. June and I gave $9.5 million to construct the building on land donated by one of our companies, Gilbert Development Company. The community raised approximately $780,000 of which my good friend Fred Shewey gave $500,000. The $780,000 was held in abeyance to use as operating capital because we knew the center would lose money in the beginning. I am thankful for all who participated in making the LJHCC a reality and for those who support it through paid memberships, event sponsorships and the like.

Over a 10-year period, we worked to bring a comprehensive health clinic to Gilbert and recently had its dedication. The creation of the health center, which was built in space that once housed two of the theaters at the LJHCC, has been a gratifying experience because it included the commitment and assistance of a number of people, including West Virginia Senator Robert C. Byrd, all of the state's medical schools and a number of benefactors. Before his death in 2010, Sen. Byrd was able to secure significant federal funding to help with its construction.

The health center has not only examination rooms, but also x-ray and laboratory facilities. It is staffed by a Gilbert-based family physician and specialists from the medical schools at WVU, Marshall and the West Virginia School of Osteopathic Medicine.

I am grateful to all who helped make the health center a reality. And I'm thankful to the physicians who have made the commitment to offer their medical expertise. Everybody in the area will have access to top-notch medical care.

Next to a loving family and a spiritual attitude, I think that a good education is the most important thing a child can have. A good education gives a child the tools to succeed. Having the necessary tools can solve so many problems, like overcoming poverty. Knowledge helps so much in creating a good self-concept and helps anyone have the confidence to try. Most people who try also succeed, if not the first time, then sooner or later. Sadly, to a large extent, we have become a society of people who expect others to give them something for nothing, and that's so unfortunate. No one can progress confidently with that kind of attitude.

We're never going to have an effective education system overall until we have some measurement of merit. A teacher's product is the education of kids, and if the kids do not gain knowledge, it's the teacher's fault, pure and simple. If the teacher does not or cannot fulfill the obligation for which he or she is being paid, then it's time to seek employment elsewhere. Let me emphasize that teachers who achieve more than expected should be paid more and held in the highest regard by their community.

Years ago, my friend Fred Shewey was on the board of education in Mingo County. The board oversaw a superintendent who was trying mightily to make the local system better. The bus drivers had become a problem and were behaving in ways that the superintendent thought were not safe. So the superintendent, with the support of board, sought to have the drivers perform more professionally, and the drivers retaliated by striking and creating a huge mess all over the county. The superintendent and board, however, did not back down. They fired every striking bus driver who refused to return to work, and it took awhile for them to find and train new bus drivers who were willing to perform to higher standards. But they achieved their desired goal.

I've learned that we must never give up our desire and willingness to try to make things better, and we must always hold ourselves and others to higher standards. We should never allow any school system to give its students less than the very best education it can.

I've been the most fortunate character. I've had a lot of friends, and I have a devoted family. Thank goodness that at a period in my life when I thought everything meaningful was totally lost, I got my life turned around and started really living. I've been a very happy man ever since.

We need spiritual guidance, we need friends, and we need love in our lives. I was reading the Bible the other night, the

13th chapter of Corinthians, which is about love. Paul was saying that you can have the world and all of the knowledge in it, but if you don't have love, you don't have anything. The saddest people I've known are the ones who have never felt a sense of love, either received or expressed. I've known good people who were pitiful because they didn't know love.

Life is complicated, and sometimes by our own actions, we make it far more so than it really needs to be. We can screw up very easily if we allow greed, passion or hatred to play roles in our decision making. I learned a long time ago that when you hate someone, you do a lot more damage to yourself than you do to the other person. I can get along with anybody, and I try to be tolerant. Hallie says I'm not nearly as tolerant as I should be and she's right. I work at it, even at my advanced age, and I'm doing better.

I so appreciate Hallie. She is a remarkable woman. She is morally straight, and her honesty and integrity are beyond reproach. She's dedicated. She had a very hard life, but says she wouldn't have it any other way since overcoming the difficulties taught her what life is really about.

I think all of us can look back and say that we learned a lot from the trying times that we lived through. I think certainly that those of us who lived through the Great Depression think a little differently than the youngsters do today because we remember how bad things were. Our kids today are unable to fathom really tough times.

It's a new world, and I'm not so sure that I like it. I'm glad that I'm not a parent of a teenager trying to make it to adulthood today because this is a tough time to be a teenager. We older folks always claim that the next generation is "going to hell in a hand basket," but I believe it may be true this time since so many things are going wrong. It is so different from when I grew up. However, I want to express strongly that there are many fine young people approaching adulthood today, and I hope that they take the mantle of leadership and work to make life better for their generation and generations to come.

Now that I coming to the end of my story, I want to emphasize to any young person reading this that you can overcome most any obstacle if you dedicate yourself wholeheartedly to work toward the goal that you've set. You'll encounter some failures, which may discourage you, but after being knocked down, get up, brush yourself off and try again. Don't give up and don't ever forget that you have the Creator who loves you, who will sustain you and who will protect you, but only if you let him into your life.

Finally, I know that I have failed to acknowledge many friends and close associates who have been important in my life and who are important to me now. My only excuse is that to list every friend and to recall every meaningful event would require a book of immense length, a near impossible task for me. I apologize, but I want those who are not recognized to know that I love you and that I have the highest regard for each of you.

INDEX

A
Abetetuba 173, 176, 184
Adair, Blind Bill 206
Adams, Russell 70
Adams Funeral Home 70
aircraft 14, 41, 56, 84, 87,
    109-10, 118-19, 129, 184,
    211-12, 227-32, 234-5, 239
airplane accident 14
airstrip 109-10, 229-30
Akers, Ray 235
Alabama 81, 94
Alara, Frank 51-2, 61-2, 102,
    108-17, 190
Alara, Madeline "Mat" 111-12,
    114-15
Alaska 203
alcohol 70, 86, 88, 243
Alcoholics Anonymous 89
American Embassy 180
American Legion Auxiliary 79
Amherst Coal Company 129
Anderson, Eddie 76
Appalachian Hardwood
    Manufacturers Association
    93
Appalachian territory 106, 186
Arab oil embargo 191
Aracoma Hotel 60
Area Redevelopment Act 102
Area Redevelopment Authority
    102-3
Arizona 185
Armstrong, Louis 130
Army Corps of Engineers 194-6
Ashland 109
Asia 188
Asunción 229
Augusta 106
Austin 215
Australia 227

B
Bank of Ieager 130
Bank of Matewan 111
Bank of Mingo 23

Barth, Anne 221
Battle of Blair Mountain 9
Beckley 204
Belcher Lumber Company 70,
    72
Belém 172, 174-5, 179, 184
Belfry 55-6
Bell Buckle 83
Benson International 120
Benson Trailer Manufacturing
    133
Bermuda 119
Bernard McGinnis Scholarship
    Fund 107
Betty Island 57
Bible 181, 248
Big Buck 218-19
Big Easy 82
B&L Furniture 115
Blairsville 41
Blankenship, Thelma 28, 30
Bluefield 104
BMW 235
Boise 240
Bolivia 179-80, 229
Boston 70-2
Brazil 87, 167-9, 171, 175-9,
    181-4, 229
Brazilian mahogany 182
Brewer, Garland 192
Brown, Bart 133
Buchannan, Rufus 47
Budig, Gene 238, 240
Buffalo Creek 94-5, 129
Bunn, Jim 214
Burch High School 55
Burger, Supreme Court Chief
    Justice Warren 123-4
Burgess, Beverly 82-3
Burgess, Blake 83
Burgess, Bruce 82-3, 192
Burgess, Debra 83
Burgess, Megan 83
Burgess Palmer, Stephanie
    82-3
Bush, President George H.W.
    215
Bush, President George W.
    215-16, 218-22, 234
Bush campaign 216-17, 221

Byrd, Preacher 60
Byrd, Senator Robert C. 213-14, 221-2, 247

C
Caffery, Jack 105, 107
California 37, 77, 188
Camp Shaw-Mi-Del-Eca 73
Campbell, Rolla D. 190
Canada 227
casket company 185
Catholic funeral 185
Catholic missionaries 169
Cayman Islands 120
Central Intelligence Agency 91
Central United Baptist Church 92
Chafin, Sheriff Don 9
Chapman, Hallie 200
Chapman, Racina 204
Charleston 91, 101, 109, 128-30, 177, 209, 211, 221, 233, 242
Charleston area 129, 186
Charleston Gazette 104, 210
Charleston Gazette and Mail 196
Chattaroy 125, 234
Chicago 8, 22, 37-9
Chicago Worlds Fair 37, 39
China 186-8, 203, 227
church 10, 30, 41, 80, 89, 111, 125, 128, 168, 181-2, 201, 203, 245
church pew factory 102-3
Cincinnati 8, 52, 113, 216
Cincinnati Reds 113, 218
Civil War 18
Clark, Doctor 73
Clay Center 221
Claypool Methodist Church 10
Cline, Debbie 181
Cline, Gary 14
Cline, Johnny 60
Cline, Lon and Iva 28, 37-9, 42
Cline, Ralph 38-9
Cline, Randy 210, 212
Cline, Retha 134
C&O Railroad 14, 100, 191

coal 4, 62, 65-6, 76, 89, 102, 111, 115, 190-3, 199, 216
business 14, 91, 98, 189, 192, 199, 216
gasification project 58
independent operators 198
industry 93, 98, 102, 196-7
miners 93, 95-7, 102, 192, 198
mines 29, 61, 76, 101, 202
mining 131, 193, 197, 199
mining laws 193
strike 93
washers 29, 193
Coleman, Betty 90, 133
Collins, Steve 235
Colorado River 117
Columbia 180
commerce department, state 208
Compton, Jim 198
Concord College 52
Concord University 52, 241
Cook, Fred 61, 63
Copacabana Hotel 167
Copenhaver, Charleston Mayor John 205
Corinthians 249
Costa Rica 84, 202
Costa Rica and Ecuador 227
Crago, George 33-42, 59-60
Crago, Norma 42
Crago's chauffeur 35
Crocket, Davey 233
Cromer, Sonny 43
Cromer's Drug Store 43
Crosby, Bing 45
Cumberland 105-6

D
D-Day 75
dance 14, 37-8, 44
DASH Coal Company 190
Davis, John 190
Davy 233
Democratic Party, state 207
Democrats 16, 207, 214
Department of Commerce 102
Depew, Fred 68
Detroit Red Wings 171

INDEX 255

Doris and Jack, Vertie's kids 5, 32
Dorsey, Dana 78
Dorsey, Tommy 44
Dotson, Junior 68
Dotson, Terry 132-3, 184
draft board 65
draftsman 64
Dudley, Lysander 238-41
Duffield 186

E

Ecuador 168-9, 179, 182
education 15-16, 57, 59, 198, 202, 206, 247-8
Effie's Place 65
Eisenhower, Dwight 215
El Paso 184-5
El Salvador 227
election 61, 79, 183, 205, 207, 213-14, 216, 222
Electoral College 216
Eller, Blaine 171, 175, 183
Ellis, George 5, 26
Ellis, Lee 60
Ellis, Maurice 38
Ellis, Ras 3, 5-6, 8-10, 12, 14-16, 26, 29-30, 60, 75, 92
Ellis, Rosa 3, 15 *(see Mom)*
Ellis Restaurant 16
Employee Stock Ownership Plan (ESOP) 133
employees 36, 84, 92, 133, 175, 185, 188, 192, 199
energy 102, 108, 125, 199
engineers 63, 170, 194, 196
England, Scott 187
environment 183, 197
environmental stewardship 196
environmentalists 197, 216
equipment 33, 63, 98, 103, 131, 175, 182, 187, 198
ESOP (Employee Stock Ownership Plan) 133
eulogy 42, 127, 130
Europe 231, 235

F

faith 41, 106, 244
Ferguson, G.A. 171-2
Fienberg, Attorney 196
fight 22-3, 51-2, 55-6, 100, 105, 201, 243
fires, forest 100-1
First Huntington National Bank 98
fish 29-30, 202
Fisher, John 189, 240-1
Fisher, Susie 241
Flamingo Beach 91
Flannery, William 96
Florida 14, 42, 115-16, 126, 171, 216, 231, 233
Flower Fund 207
Fogelsong, General Robert "Doc" 234-6
Fogelsong, Mary 234, 236-7
football 7, 16, 51, 54-7, 61, 74, 236
Ford, President Gerald 215
Founding Fathers 20
Fox, Alton 17
Fox, Pierce 50, 207
Fox, Roy 16
France 203, 227
friends 41, 48, 76, 84, 96, 106, 114, 125, 127, 167-8, 206, 208-9, 213, 222, 234, 245, 248, 250
friendship 15, 35, 41, 67, 82, 107, 129, 222
furniture industry 103-4, 186-8

G

Gainesville 14
Gander 235
Gary in McDowell County 105
Gay, Harry S. 127
Gay Mining Company 127
Gee, Gordon 120, 123-4, 240-1
Georgia Pacific Corporation 106-7
Germany 177, 227, 234-5
Ghost Ship 88, 183
Gibraltar 203, 227

Gilbert 7-8, 10-11, 13-14, 16, 21-6, 30-1, 33, 37-9, 41-3, 45-8, 56-60, 68-71, 76-8, 81-2, 94, 98-9, 128, 130, 186, 190, 194, 207-8, 211-12, 231-3, 245-6
   Bank and Trust 131
   High School 53, 55, 57-9, 83
   High School Reunion 52
   Kiwanis Club 128
   Lumber Company 81, 106
   Presbyterian Church 80, 181-2
Gilco Lumber 187
Girls State 79
Glenn, Senator John 241
goal 69-70, 81, 103, 198, 248, 250
God 80, 177, 189
Golden Arrow 48
Golden Eagle 50
golf 116, 119, 126, 203
Goodman, Benny 44
Gore, Vice-President Al 216
government, state 197, 206
grade school 3, 15, 18-19, 30
Great Depression 10, 14, 33, 45, 100, 249
Greece 203
Greenbrier, The 100-1, 116, 177
Greenbrier Military School 73-4
Greenbrier Presbytery 196
Greenbrier River 73
Greenland 227
Grey, Zane 18-19
Grimmet, Eddie 192
Grundy 55
Guatemala 181-3, 227
Guatemalan mill 182
Guyan Restaurant 69
Guyandotte River 14, 28-9, 57, 77, 194
Guyandotte Valley 38
Gypsies 24-5

H

Haden, Judge Charles 195
Haiti 227
Hallie 20, 129-30, 132, 184, 200-4, 216-20, 222, 234-7, 241, 249

Hallie's restaurant 201
Hamilton
   Lawson 127-30, 197, 209-10
   Lefty 112
   Tripp 128
Hampden Coal Company 189, 236
Hannah, Everett 188
hardwoods 174, 186, 188
Harlan 232
Harless, Hannah 89
Harless, Jamey 81, 88, 90-1
Harless, Kitty 89
Harless, Maureen 81, 84
Harless, Paula 89
Harless, Sjon 91
Harless, Tripp 91
Harvey, Bill 231
Hatfield, Bob 51
Hatfield, Devil Anse 51
Hatfield, Dr H.D. 75
Hatfield, Frank 51, 61
Hatfield, Junior 78
Hatfield, Margaret 52
Hatfield, Sid 13
Hatfield, Wirt 21, 23, 30, 205
Hatfield and McCoy Trail 189
Hatfield's Restaurant 128
Haught, James 104-5
Hawaii 132
Hayes, Marshall University President Robert B. 242
Hazard 109
Henderson, Cam 54
high school 3, 5, 7, 14-15, 18, 40, 43, 46-8, 52, 54-6, 79, 82, 192, 198, 236
   new Mingo Central 57-8
high school diploma 241
high school graduating class 53
highway 3, 8, 10, 15, 95, 113, 125, 184, 208, 224-6
Holt & Bugbee Company 70
home 3, 5, 10-13, 15-16, 19, 29-31, 38-9, 46, 49-51, 66, 70, 73, 75, 78, 81, 86, 94-6, 99, 104, 109, 111, 114, 125, 200-1, 245
Hontas, George 53
Hontas, Lena 53

INDEX 257

Hoover Dam   117
Horsepen   48, 199
Horsepen Bridge   127
Horton, Margaret Akers   235
Houston   177, 183
Huff Creek   9
Huffman, John   231, 235
Huntington   14, 75, 99, 105, 109, 179, 190, 202, 225
Huntington State Hospital   86
Hylton, Tracy   197

I

I-74   58
Iaeger   13, 49, 130, 224-5
Iceland   227, 235
Ida   67-8
Idaho   240
Indiana   38, 227
Indianapolis   8
Indonesia   186
International Industries, Inc   121, 134, 244
Internet   19, 21
Iraq   222
Ireland   227
Isaban and War Eagle   48
Isaiah   181
Isom, Roy   66
Italy   203, 227

J

Jack Benny Program   76
Jack Dempsey-Gene Tunney fight   22
Jackson Kelly law firm   195-6
James River Coal Company   92
Japan   227
Jefferson Standard Life Insurance Company   59
Jenkins   52, 111
Joan C. Edwards School of Medicine   179
jobs   11, 14, 30, 34, 61-5, 68, 82, 94, 102-3, 121, 129, 133, 173, 177, 179, 182, 192, 197, 205-7, 231
Johnny Cake Mountain   224

Johnson, Mr.   94, 96-7
Jones, Charlie   129, 209
Jones, Gene   233
Jones, Mary Lou   233-4
Jones family   197
Judy   75-83, 223
Jumacris Mining   115, 189, 192
June   57, 61, 65-6, 68, 73-4, 76, 78, 80-2, 86-8, 115, 117, 167-8, 181, 199-200, 246
jungle   169-70, 174, 179, 229
Justice   40, 65, 124, 202
Justice, Jim   197
Justice, Morris   76
Justonian Restaurant   200, 202

K

Kanawha River   129
Kansas   240
KDKA   22
Keflavik   235
Kelly, John   66
Kennedy, Bobby   118
Kennedy, President John F.   102
Kennedy, Thomas   94
Kentucky   47, 52, 55, 60, 80, 105-6, 109, 111, 133, 231-2
Kermit   115, 206
kickbacks   61, 207
Kimberling Collieries   76
King Coal Highway   58
Kirby, Mr.   66-8
Kirk, Maurice   81
Kissinger, Henry   220
Kiwanis Club   78, 123, 200
Knoxville   106, 109-10

L

La Paz   179-80
Lambert, Carl   131
Lambert, June   94-5
Larry   61, 73-4, 76-7, 80-1, 83-6, 88, 90-1, 116-18, 167-9, 176, 183, 185, 245-6
Laura J   129
Lawson, Brooks   106, 122-6, 239
Lester, Alex   60
Lester, Oma   60

Lewis, John L. 93, 97
Lewisburg 74
Lexington 231
Lincoln County 94
Linder, Jr., Carl 217-18
loan 40-1, 77, 98-100, 105-6, 129, 131-2, 134
   uncollateralized personal 105
Lockwood, Maurice 81
Logan 36, 41, 60, 82, 92, 127, 200, 203, 226
Logan County 9-10, 95, 129
loggers, Brazilian 173-4
Lone Ranger 37
Lorado Mining 94-5, 98
Lord 13, 80, 244
Lord's Prayer 181
Lord's wisdom 244
Los Angeles 245
Louis, Joe 171
Louisville 47, 59
luck 15, 29, 191
lucky 42-3, 54, 98, 118, 228
lumber 66, 70-2, 81, 91, 103, 169, 174, 177-8, 182-3, 185, 229-30
lumber business 14, 68, 88, 100, 105, 167, 171, 179, 186, 188-9
Lynch 105
Lynchburg 11, 13

M

Madison Square Garden 171
Man 23-4, 74, 94-6, 106, 119, 128, 226
Manaus 229
Marshall, Chief Justice John 126
Marshall College 54
Marshall University 54, 107, 179, 202, 241-2
Matewan 55, 65-6, 110-11, 236
Matewan National 130
Maurice, John 65
McDowell County 105, 233
McGinnis, Bernard 99, 101, 105, 107
McGinnis, Muriel "Moo" 107

McGinnis family 107
McGlothlin, Cotton 228-32
Meade Chevrolet dealership 132
Meade's Shopping Center 194
Melville 18
Memphis 117-18, 185
Miami 80
Miller, Buck 171-3, 175-6, 183
millionaire 46
Milton, brother 14
Mineral Wells 133
Mingo County 48, 61, 202, 206-7, 212, 234, 237, 248
   Board of Education 57, 206
Mingo-Wyoming Coal Land Company 190
Mobile 81, 83-5, 89, 91, 117, 126, 174, 183, 228
Mollette, Brett 204
Mollette, Ryan 204
Mollohan, Representative Robert 206
Mom 3-14, 16, 18, 24-7, 30, 33, 46-9, 60, 74-5, 92
Momma Jean 129
money 7-8, 26, 34, 38-9, 43, 45-6, 51-2, 57, 69-71, 76, 88, 99-100, 103-4, 116, 131-2, 191, 198, 202, 205, 208, 211, 222, 229, 238-9, 246
Montgomery, Emma 76, 86
moonshine 26, 48
Moore, Jr., Governor Arch 238
Moore, Leff 189
Morgan, Norman 80
Morgantown 211, 238-9
Mount Rushmore 203
Mountain Club 113
Mountain State 102
mountains 4, 24, 39, 193, 224, 232, 245
Mounts, Jake 69
movement, environmental 102, 193
movie 49-50, 66, 76, 88, 183, 201
Mullen, Billy 222-3
Mullen, Shari 222
Murfreesboro 83
Murphy, Sharon 134

INDEX

N
National Seating and Dimension Company 103
Nehlen, Don 211-12
Nehrt, Leo 227
Nester, Roy 50
New Orleans 81-2
New York Rangers 171
New Zealand 227
Newfoundland 235
Nickelodeon 44
Nixon, President Richard 215
Nolan Airport 109
Norfolk 188
Norfolk Southern Corporation 100, 104, 186
Norfolk Southern Railroad 11
Norris Grain Company 171-2
North and South Dakota 227
North Carolina 103, 126, 185-6

O
Oceana 208
O'Connor, Supreme Court Justice Sandra Day 124
Ohio 52-3, 111, 129, 211, 219, 241
Ohio State University 241
Old Stone Presbyterian Church in Lewisburg 128
Oldsmobile 82, 224
Oliverio, Moises 172
Omar 49-51
outhouses 4, 18, 29
Oval Office 222-3

P
Panama 227
Parade Day 74
Paraguay 229
Paris 237
Parkersburg 120
partners 31, 44, 46, 69, 171, 190, 201, 243
partnership 56
Paul the Apostle 249
Peake, Charley 54
Peake Jr., Charles 182
Peck, Officer 48-9
Pennsylvania 22, 41-2
Pensacola 126
Perry, Ray 47
Phipps, Lowell 58-9
Phipps, Miss Anne 78
Phipps, Ruth 125, 134, 177
Pigeon Creek 40, 103
Pikeville College 241
pilots 14, 107, 119, 228-9, 231-5
Pittsburgh 22
Plymouth, family 23-6, 32-3
Pocahontas Land Corporation 107, 186, 189
police, state 40, 212
politicians 8, 61, 209
politics 8, 61, 95, 125, 205, 209
Port Amherst 91
Portugal 186, 203, 227
Portuguese 87, 167, 171, 173, 175
Potlatch 183
Potter, Tom 215
Presbyterian Church USA 196
Preservati, Karen 132
Preservati, Richard "Dick" 131-2
Prestonsburg 231
Princeton 41, 233
Proctorville 111
Provident Bank and American Financial Group 218
Puerto Rico 227

R
radio 21-3, 30, 37-8, 75, 87, 110, 205
Raines, Bob 189
Ramstein Air Base 234-5
Randolph, Senator Jennings 242
Randolph County 122
Rawl 111
Reagan, President Ronald 215-16
reclamation 197
Red Jacket Consolidated Coal & Coke Co. 61, 63-6, 68, 108, 205
regulations 193, 197
Renison, Tom 233

reporters 105, 180
Reynolds, Mercer 217-18
ringer, bringing in a 55
Ritter Lumber Company 66
Rivers and Harbors Act 195
road 6, 8, 15, 18, 32-3, 69, 79,
  89, 95, 125, 171, 189, 202
Robinson, George 179, 181-2
Robinson, Lilly 181
Rochester (Eddie Anderson) 76
Rockefeller, Jay 58, 209-12
Rockefeller, Senator Jay 209
Roderfield 225
Rometta, Coach 55
Rove, Karl 222
Ruby Memorial Hospital 204
Rutledge, Tim 181

S

Sammons, Terry 184, 192
San Lorenzo 168-9
Santa Cruz 229
Savannah office 89
sawmill 14, 68-9, 76, 95, 99,
  168-9, 171, 175, 194, 201-2
school 7, 12, 15-16, 18-19, 28,
  37, 43, 48, 58, 73-4, 80, 175
  bus 48
  library 19
  system 16, 248
Schroeder, John 105
Secret Service 216
Seiler, Fanny 210
Senate Select Committee on
  Small Business 93
Shanghai 187
Shelbyville 83
Shewey, Christine 60, 115-16,
  121-2
Shewey, Fred 14, 60, 84, 102,
  115-22, 126, 168-9, 190, 206,
  228-9
shooting off the solid 191
shotgun, automatic 90
slate 193-5, 207
Small Business Administration
  98-100
Smith, Hulett 104, 208-9

South Africa 199
South America 81, 167, 174,
  177, 183, 203, 227-9
South and Central America 182
Southern Illinois University 56
southern West Virginia 4, 54,
  100, 102, 105, 131, 133, 189,
  192, 197
Spain 186, 227
Sparkman, Senator John 94
Spratt, Audrey 50
Spratt, Rouhier 48
Sprigg Country Club 112-13
Star Spangled Banner 129
State Band 78
state road commission 207
Sternwheel Regatta 129
Stillman College 241
Stinson, Willis 53
Stirrat 50
Suriname and French Guiana
  227

T

Taiwan 187-8
Taplin Field 106
Tatum, Shorty 11-13
Taylor, Maurice 195
teachers 18, 20, 27-8, 41, 47,
  51-3, 56-7, 59-60, 78, 207,
  247-8
technology 20, 22, 188, 199, 206
television 19-21, 215, 219
Tennessee Walking Horses 83
Texas 177, 183-4, 215, 218, 222
Thompson, Everett 125-7
timber 105-7, 169, 174
Time magazine 241
Titusville 231
Tocantins River 173
Toothman, Fred 191
Tsutras, Frank 102
Turner, Amy 222
Turner, Reverend Chris 222-3
Twain, Mark 19, 28
Twentieth Street Bank 99, 105
typhoid fever 26-8

INDEX

U

UMWA 93-4
Underwood, Cecil 100-1, 115, 205-6, 208, 213
Underwood, Governor Cecil 101
union 93-4, 97-8, 103
University of Charleston 130, 241
University of Kansas 240
University of Kentucky 80
University of Miami 80
U.S. Air Forces Europe (USAFE) 234-5
U.S. District Court 195
U.S. Steel Corp. 100, 105, 107, 131, 225
U.S. Supreme Court 124

V

Venezuela 183
Verner 48
Vertie (Alberta) 5, 32-3
Vietnam 183, 186
Vietnam veteran 233
Vinciquerra, Elizabeth Sparks 57
Virgil, interpreter 177-8
Virginia 11, 55, 98, 186, 188

W

Walden, Dr. John 179
Walker, Dr. 33
Walls, Larry 14
Walters Construction Company 11, 178
War Eagle 48
Ward, Miss 9
Washington 93, 123-4, 212, 222
Weathers, Colonel Richard 235
Webb School 83
Welch 11, 42, 66, 107
Welch Hospital 76
West Hamlin 178-9
West Virginia 8, 19, 36, 52, 54, 58, 72, 75, 100-2, 104, 133, 175, 178, 189, 197, 206, 215-16, 220-1, 227, 234, 238
West Virginia Coal Association 91
West Virginia Forestry Association 100
West Virginia University 21, 80, 83, 122, 187, 204, 211-12, 234, 238, 240-1
  College of Law 189
  Marching Band 238
West Virginia University Foundation 238
Western Pocahontas Corporation 191
Western Pocahontas Land Corp 100
Weyerhaeuser 183
White, Catherine 92
White, Doris 48
White, Jo Ann 222
White, Lacy 96
White, Reverend Glenn 92
White House 124, 220-2
Whitt, Mike 189
Williamson 40, 102, 114, 122, 125, 130, 205, 239
Williamson Presbyterian Church 125
Williamson YMCA 108
Wingo, Bud 47
Wirt's radio 21-2, 37
Wise, Governor Bob 215
Wise, Representative Bob 213
Woolridge, Bob 40
Workforce Retraining Program 103
World War II 8, 64, 177
World Wide Web 19
Worldwide Equipment Corp 132-3
WVU-Tech 204
Wyoming 209
Wyoming County 48, 210

Y

Yellowstone Park 203